# The Big Book of Puzzles

**Writers:**

Mark Danna

Helene Hovanec

Vicky Shiotsu

**Illustrators (mazes):**

Dave Roberts

Marylin Roberts

**Illustrators:**

Lisa Covington

Giuseppe Conserti

Publications International, Ltd.

# Hello, Parents and Teachers-

The pages of *Super Brain Builders: The Big Book of Puzzles* are jammed with an exciting collection of puzzles, word games, trivia quizzes, and much more. These puzzles will help kids improve their logical thinking skills, build their vocabulary, and practice what they've learned in school—all while having a blast!

The puzzles in this book are perfect for challenging kids. Beginners will love working on puzzles that are at just the right level, intermediates will eat up the food for thought in the middle sections, and advanced puzzlers will love running the mental marathons near the end of the book.

Many educators agree that puzzles and games are among the best ways to engage children in the thinking process. Your mission is to get them started on the journey toward learning. So give them this book, and turn them loose on puzzling.

## Hey Kids! Are You Ready to Have Some Fun?

Here's the easiest question in *Super Brain Builders: The Big Book of Puzzles*: What's the best way to get the most out of this huge book of puzzles? The answer: Read this page first!

- *Super Brain Builders: The Big Book of Puzzles* is sorted from easiest to most difficult. The easiest puzzles are in the front of the book, and the ones that make your head spin are in the back. If you get bored, feel free to move ahead. If you start feeling a little frustrated, you can always back up.

- You can find the answers to every puzzle at the back of the book. Just be sure you give each puzzle a fair try before peeking at the answers—it's not called *Super Brain Builders: The Big Book of Puzzles* for nothing, and you want to be sure you give your brain the full workout before calling for help.

- No matter what puzzle you're working on—whether you solve it in a snap or get hung up on it for what seems like ages—the most important thing to remember is to have fun! If a particular puzzle isn't fun for you, skip it! No sweat.

Now you're ready to get started! Every day is a great day for puzzles, so don't wait for a rainy day. (It will just get the pages wet anyway!)

# What's at the Theater?

There's a letter missing from each word below. Each word refers to something at a theater. Use one of the five letters we've given you. After you've used one, you can cross it off because each letter will be used only once.

S E A V C

1. MO__IE

2. POP__ORN

3. __ODA

4. TICK__TS

5. C__NDY

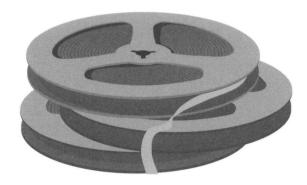

Answers on page 267

# Out of Place

Cross off the one word that doesn't belong with the others in the group.

1.  Green
    ~~Plane~~
    Purple
    Pink

2.  Two
    Four
    ~~Watch~~
    Eight

3.  ~~Cat~~
    Robin
    Sparrow
    Dove

4.  Cereal
    Milk
    Banana
    ~~Book~~

5.  Train
    Car
    ~~House~~
    Boat

6.  Mom
    ~~Family~~
    Dad
    Brother

Answers on page 267

# True or False

Read each sentence. If it's true, circle the letter in the TRUE column. If it's false, circle the letter in the FALSE column. Then read the circled letters from top to bottom to find the name of a planet in our solar system.

|  | TRUE | FALSE |
|---|---|---|
| A computer is an animal. | J | N |
| A watch tells time. | E | U |
| 2 + 2 = 4 | P | T |
| All flowers are pink. | I | T |
| E is a vowel. | U | T |
| A dime has a square shape. | E | N |
| December is the last month of the year. | E | R |

Answers on page 267

# Bee Quick

Follow the bee through the cluster of flowers to gather pollen, then get to the beehive in a hurry.

Answer on page 267

# For the Birds

Place each bird into the grid. There are some letters already in place to get you flying.

**3 Letters**
Owl

**4 Letters**
Dove
Lark

**5 Letters**
Eagle
Goose
Robin

**6 Letters**
Pigeon

**8 Letters**
Bluebird
Parakeet

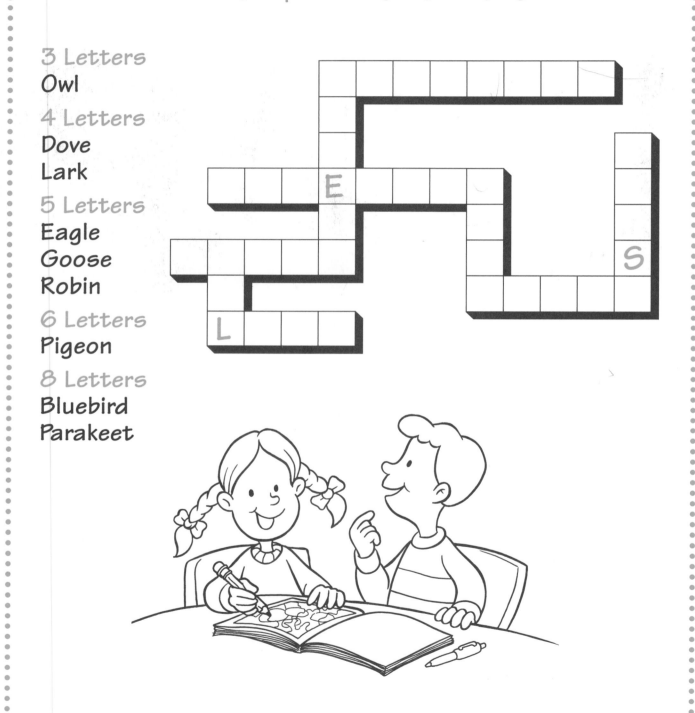

Answers on page 267

# A Matter of Taste

Color in each box with a > in it (but NOT with a <), and you'll find something that may be salty or made of chocolate.

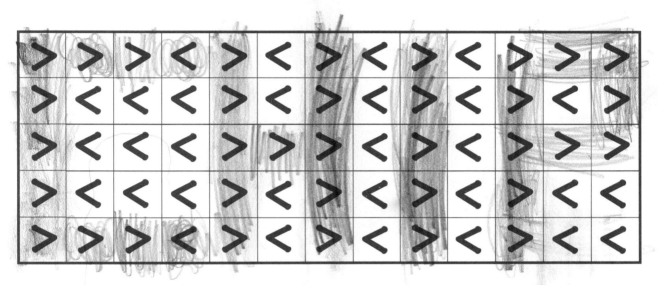

chip

Answer on page 267

# Ann E. Gram

Sometimes the letters of a word can be put in a different order to spell a new word, like *RATS* and *STAR*. This is called an *anagram*. Draw a line from a word in Column 1 to a word in Column 2 that uses the same letters.
We did one for you.

| Column 1 | Column 2 |
|----------|----------|
| NEST | TRAP |
| SHOE | DENS |
| ENDS | FILE |
| LOSE | SENT |
| PART | BLOW |
| BOWL | SOLE |
| LIFE | HOSE |

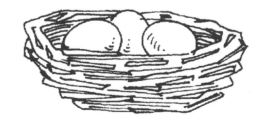

Answers on page 267

# High Flying

Connect the dots 1 through 39 to complete the picture.

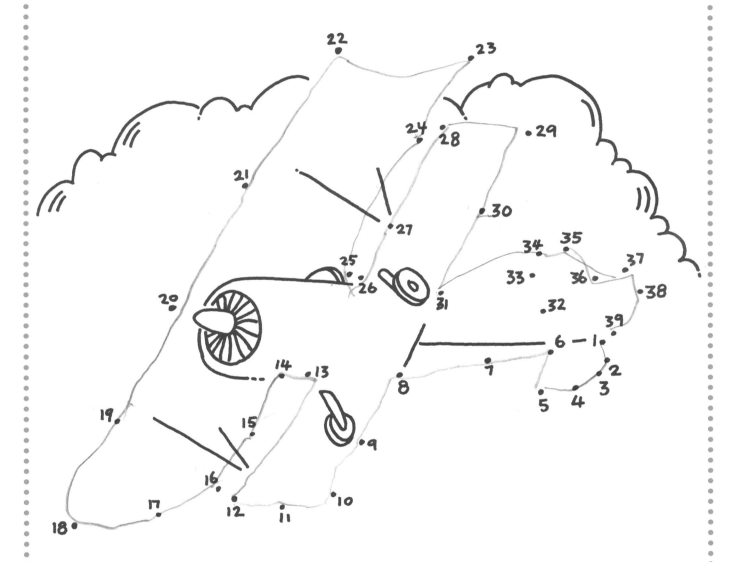

# Wild Cats

Place each wild cat into the grid. There are some letters already in place to get you running.

**4 Letters**
Lion

**5 Letters**
Tiger

**6 Letters**
Cougar
Jaguar

**7 Letters**
Cheetah
Leopard
Panther

# "E" Words

The 12 words in this list all start with the letter E. Each word is also hidden in the grid. Look across or down and circle each word as you find it. Then cross the word off the list. Eagle is circled in the grid and crossed off the list to get you started.

Eagle
Earth
Easter
Ends

Energy
Engine
Enter
Erase

Even
Every
Exam
Eyes

| E | A | G | L | E | E | E | Q |
| A | E | Z | E | V | A | N | E |
| S | V | E | N | E | R | G | Y |
| T | E | X | D | N | T | I | E |
| E | R | A | S | E | H | N | S |
| R | Y | M | E | N | T | E | R |

Answers on page 267

# Step by Step

Name each picture, and write it in the grid making sure that you match up the numbers. The end of one word will be the start of the next word.

# Cross It Out

Follow the cross-out instructions for the letters in the grid. Then, take the leftover letters and put them in the blank spaces below. Go from left to right and top to bottom, and you will answer this riddle:

## What goes up but never comes down?

Cross out 3 B's
Cross out 4 C's
Cross out 2 D's
Cross out 4 F's
Cross out 3 H's
Cross out 2 I's
Cross out 3 J's
Cross out 2 K's
Cross out 3 L's
Cross out 4 M's
Cross out 3 N's
Cross out 3 P's
Cross out 2 Q's
Cross out 4 S's

| B | Y | J | F | F | F | F |
|---|---|---|---|---|---|---|
| I | B | J | I | N | N | O |
| U | P | B | S | S | N | J |
| Q | P | S | S | R | L | H |
| Q | P | K | A | L | C | H |
| D | M | K | L | C | G | C |
| D | M | E | M | M | C | H |

Riddle answer:  your age

Answer on page 267

# Fruit Salad

All 8 fruits in the word list are hidden in the berry-shaped grid below. Look across, down, and diagonally. Circle each word in the grid as you find it, and cross it off the word list. We found *Banana* to get you started.

### Word list

- ~~Banana~~
- ~~Berry~~
- ~~Grape~~
- ~~Melon~~
- ~~Orange~~
- ~~Peach~~
- ~~Pear~~
- Plum

Answers on page 267

# Lost Planet Maze

Can you help the explorer get back to his ship while the alien's back is turned?

Answer on page 267

# What's Your Number?

Write each number word in the grid. We put a few letters in place to get you started.

**3 Letters**
One
Six
Ten
Two

**4 Letters**
Five
Four
Nine

**5 Letters**
Eight
Seven
Three

Answers on page 268

# Works of Art

Use the letters of the word art to complete each word below.

1.  t r a Y

2.  S t a r

3.  t r a i N

4. 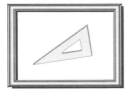 H E N t e

5.  E a r t H

6.  F E t h E r

7.  t r i g N G L E

Answers on page 268

# Tiny Creatures

Write one of the six letters in an empty space to complete the name of each tiny creature you might see in the park. Cross off each letter as you use it.

B M A W S F

1. ___ NT
2. ___ EE
3. ___ LY
4. ___ OTH
5. ___ NAIL
6. ___ ASP

# Gigantic Creatures

Write one of the six letters in an empty space to complete the name of each gigantic creature you might see in the zoo. Cross off each letter as you use it.

G H E P R C

1. ___ YTHON
2. ___ ROCODILE
3. ___ IPPOPOTAMUS
4. ___ HINOCEROS
5. ___ IRAFFE
6. ___ LEPHANT

Answers on page 268

# Picture Crossword

Look at the pictures on this page, and name each one.
Then write the word in the correct numbered spaces.
Be sure to check to see if the word should be
written across or down.

## Across

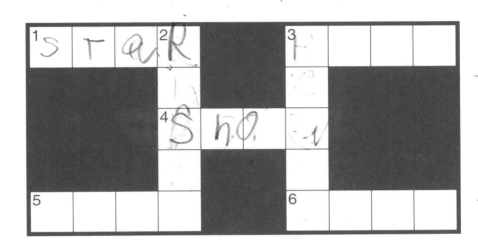

1.

3.

4.

5.

6.

## Down

2.

3.

Answers on page 268

# It's a Hot One Today

All 10 words in the word list are hidden in the sun-shaped grid below. Look across, down, and diagonally to find these words about the weather. Circle each word in the grid as you find it, and then cross it off the word list. We circled Wet to get you started.

**Word list**

Cloudy
Damp
Hail
Hot
Lightning
Sleet
Storm
Thunder
~~Wet~~
Wind

Answers on page 268

# Bible Fun

Find each person in the word list in one of the sentences below. Each person is found in the Bible. Then circle each one as you find it. We found the first one for you and crossed it off the list.

**Word list**

~~Abel~~
Adam
Amos
Esther
Eve
Lydia
Mary
Paul
Peter
Ruth

1. Please bring a bell to school.
2. They went to the spa ultimately.
3. The car got stuck in a rut here in town.
4. Seven can play this game at home.
5. The ape terrified the children.
6. Britney owned the only diary.
7. On your nose is a mosquito.
8. Ma, rye bread or white bread?
9. There should be no cracks in a dam.
10. My cat teases the rabbit at night.

Answers on page 268

# Word Play

Place one letter in each blank space to spell a word that means the opposite of the word on the left. Then read down to answer this riddle: What is the happiest state?

| | |
|---|---|
| Divide | __ U L T I P L Y |
| Below | __ B O V E |
| Smooth | __ O U G H |
| Old | __ O U N G |
| Tighten | __ O O S E N |
| Present | __ B S E N T |
| Wide | __ A R R O W |
| Easy | __ I F F I C U L T |

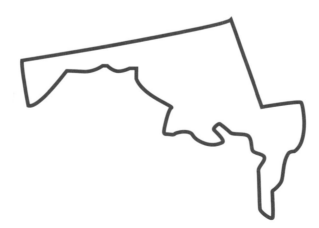

Answers on page 268

# Getting There

Put each vehicle word into the only spot in the grid where it will fit. Start by using the letters that are already in the grid. One word will lead to another until the grid is filled.

**3 Letters**
Bus
Car

**4 Letters**
Boat

**5 Letters**
Plane
Train
Truck

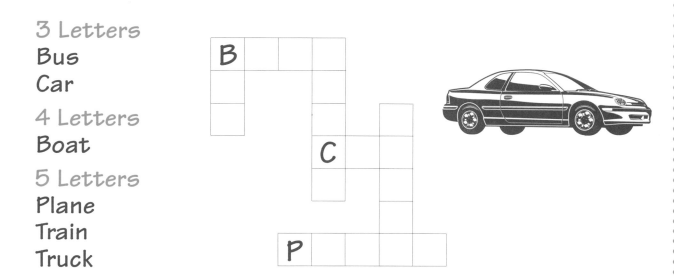

This list has the names of 5 states that people could travel to. Put each state name into the only spot in the grid where it will fit. Start with the only 5-letter state, and place it into the only 5-letter spot.

**4 Letters**
Iowa
Utah

**5 Letters**
Maine

**6 Letters**
Alaska
Hawaii

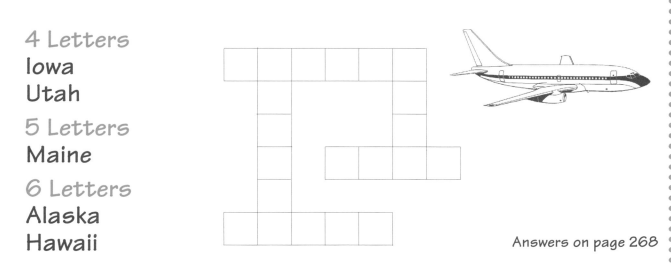

Answers on page 268

# A Classroom Puzzle

Write the names of the pictures on the lines to complete the puzzle. Each picture shows something you will find in a classroom.

1.  C __ __ __ __

2.  __ L __ __ __

3.  __ A __ __ __

4.  __ __ S __

5.  S __ __ __ __ __ __

6.  R __ __ __ __ __

7.  __ O __ __

8.  __ __ O __ __

9.  M __ __ __ __ __

Answers on page 268

# Ant Words

The word ANT is part of lots of other words. Fill in each blank space with a letter to make words that fit the definitions.

| | | |
|---|---|---|
| __ A N T __ | = | Needs a belt |
| __ __ A N T | = | Grows in a pot |
| A __ __ __ N __ T | = | Not for |
| __ __ A N __ T | = | Goes around the sun |
| A N T __ __ __ __ | = | Old furniture |

# Ruff!

The word DOG is part of lots of other words. Fill in each blank space with a letter to make words that fit the definitions.

| | | |
|---|---|---|
| D O __ G __ | = | Flour and milk |
| D O __ G __ | = | To avoid a ball |
| D __ O __ G __ __ | = | Dry spell |
| __ __ __ D O __ __ G | = | Loosening |
| __ __ __ __ D __ O __ G | = | Lacking restraint |

Answers on page 268

# Letters in Colors

One letter was added to each word in Column 1 to make a new word in Column 2. Find the added letter, and write it in Column 3. Then read down to find a color.

| Column 1 | Column 2 | Column 3 |
|----------|----------|----------|
| RAN | RANG | ____ |
| TIP | TRIP | ____ |
| HAT | HEAT | ____ |
| BAR | BEAR | ____ |
| EAT | NEAT | ____ |

Now find another color.

| Column 1 | Column 2 | Column 3 |
|----------|----------|----------|
| EARL | EARLY | ____ |
| TWIN | TWINE | ____ |
| BACK | BLACK | ____ |
| PEAR | PEARL | ____ |
| PINT | POINT | ____ |
| OMEN | WOMEN | ____ |

Answers on page 268

# Add a Letter

Below is a list of three-letter words. If you add the same letter to the beginning of each word,
you get a four-letter word. What is the letter?

G OLD

H EAR

D ART

C HAT

F ILL

H RIM

S HIS

P AIL

S ORE

M ASK

Answers on page 268

# Step by Step

Name each picture, and write it in the grid. Make sure you match the numbers so you write it in the right place. The end of one word will be the beginning of the next word.

1.

2.

3.

4.

5.

6.

7.

8.

The grid contains: 1. bear, 2. rope, 3. eggs, 4. ship, 5. pail, 6. lamb, 7. book, 8. keys

Answers on page 268

# Jurassic Jerry

Travel back in time through a dinosaur's body!

IN

OUT

Answer on page 268

# G Is for Guessing

How many things can you find that start with the letter *G*? Finding 20 would be GOOD. Finding 25 would be GREAT!

Answers on page 269

# A Shirt Riddle

Here's a short riddle—or is it a shirt riddle? What button do you have that you can never unbutton? For the answer, move the letters on the list to the numbered spaces below. Then read from 1 to 15.

B goes to spaces 5 and 10.

E goes to space 6.

L goes to spaces 7 and 8.

N goes to space 15.

O goes to spaces 2 and 14.

R goes to space 4.

T goes to spaces 12 and 13.

U goes to spaces 3 and 11.

Y goes to spaces 1 and 9.

Y O U R B E L L Y B U T T O N
1 2 3 4 5 6 7 8 9 10 11 12 13 14 15

Answer on page 269

# Name Game

Each name will fit into just one spot in the grid below. Start by putting the only 8-letter name into the only 8-letter spot. Then use the letters that are already in the grid to guide you as you fit each name into its proper place.

**4 Letters**
Emma
Kate
Lynn
Mark

**5 Letters**
Ethan
Lewis
Suzie

**6 Letters**
Ashley
Hannah

**7 Letters**
Abigail
Matthew
Michael

**8 Letters**
Samantha

Answers on page 269

# Vowels in the City

According to the 2000 U.S. census, the following cities had the most people in the United States. Fill in the missing vowels to complete the name of each city, and cross off each vowel as you use it. The cities are listed from largest to smallest.

A A A A A A A A A E E E E E E
I I I I I I O O O O O O O O O O U

1. N _e_ W Y _O_ R K
2. L _ S _ N G _ L _ S
3. C H _ C _ G _
4. H _ _ S T _ N
5. P H _i_ L _i_ D _a_ L P H _i_ _a_
6. P H _ _ N _ X
7. S _ N D _ _ G _
8. S _ N _ N T _ N _ _
9. D _ L L _ S
10. D _ T R _ _ T

Answers on page 269

# A Trail of Threes

Help the tiger get back to the jungle. Make a path by coloring the spaces that have multiples of 3 (such as 12 and 24). (Hint: Here's a quick way to tell if a number is a multiple of 3. The sum of its digits will be divisible by 3!)

| 3 | 12 | 27 | 15 | 24 |
|---|---|---|---|---|

| 4 | 2 | 10 | 7 | 11 | 8 | 6 |
|---|---|---|---|---|---|---|
| 13 | 16 | 48 | 39 | 9 | 30 | 21 |
| 20 | 23 | 33 | 26 | 14 | 5 | 29 |
| 45 | 36 | 42 | 32 | 90 | 93 | 18 |
| 60 | 37 | 40 | 46 | 69 | 61 | 99 |
| 66 | 54 | 63 | 72 | 96 | 70 | |

Answer on page 269

# State Lines

Put each state name into the grid in alphabetical order. Then read down the starred column to find the name of another state. Cross off each word after you write it into the grid.

**OHIO**

KENTUCKY

**UTAH**

MISSOURI

**ALASKA**

**OKLAHOMA**

PENNSYLVANIA

**COLORADO**

**MAINE**

# Hidden Numbers

A number word is hidden in each sentence below. Underline the number words, and write them on the lines. The first one has been done for you.

1. Brent won a ticket to a football game. _____two_____

2. I like to go on walks even when it rains. _____

3. Tell Jan that I'll call her if I've got her book. _____

4. Dr. Desi x-rays people at the clinic. _____

5. Matt enjoys reading comic books. _____

6. We hope to ride a sleigh today. _____

7. The baker put a tasty bun in every box. _____

8. The basket is filled with reeds. _____

9. I will go next week when I feel better. _____

10. If our plan doesn't work, we'll have to give up. _____

Answers on page 269

# Parachute Words

Each word in the list is made up of the letters in the word *Parachute*. Can you place each word into the grid in the only spot where it will fit? Start with the letters that are already in the grid, and work from there. Cross off each word as you place it in the grid.

**3 Letters**
Car
Put
Rap

**4 Letters**
Harp
Part
Tear

**5 Letters**
Acute
Crate
Earth
Heart
Teach

**6 Letters**
Carpet
Teacup

**7 Letters**
Chapter

Answers on page 269

# Mystery Words

**1.** Cross out the letters in the word *BIRD*. Unscramble the remaining letters to write the name of a bird.

| I | E | G |
|---|---|---|
| L | B | A |
| R | D | E |

— — — — —

**2.** Cross out the letters in the word *TREE*. Unscramble the remaining letters to write the name of a tree.

| L | E | A |
|---|---|---|
| T | E | R |
| M | P | E |

— — — — —

**3.** Cross out the letters in the word *DOG*. Unscramble the remaining letters to write the name of a dog.

| I | O | D |
|---|---|---|
| O | C | L |
| L | G | E |

— — — — — —

**4.** Cross out the letters in the word *FRUIT*. Unscramble the remaining letters to write the name of a fruit.

| F | L | T |
|---|---|---|
| M | R | U |
| I | U | P |

— — — —

**5.** Cross out the letters in the word *FISH*. Unscramble the remaining letters to write the name of a fish.

| R | H | U |
|---|---|---|
| F | T | S |
| O | I | T |

— — — — —

**6.** Cross out the letters in the word *SPORT*. Unscramble the remaining letters to write the name of a sport.

| G | S | L |
|---|---|---|
| O | F | O |
| T | P | R |

— — — —

Answers on page 269

# Change to Sport

The made-up words below will become a type of sport if you change the underlined letter to a new letter. Write the new words in the blank spaces.

1. <u>W</u>OCCER = _Soccer_
2. BA<u>K</u>EBALL = _basketball_
3. FOOT<u>T</u>ALL = _football_
4. T<u>O</u>NNIS = _tennis_
5. GOL<u>P</u> = _golf_
6. B<u>I</u>SKETBALL = _____

# Puzzling Animals

Put one of the words from Column 1 into a blank space in Column 2 to make an animal word on each line.

| Column 1 | Column 2 |
|----------|----------|
| U S | __ __ T |
| B E | P __ __ Y |
| A N | R O B __ __ |
| U P | __ __ A V E R |
| I N | M O __ __ E |
| O N | P O R C _i_ _p_ I N E |

Answers on page 269

# Good Dog

All eight dog words in the world list below are hidden in the grid. Look across, backward, up, or down. Circle the words in the grid, and then cross them off the list as you go.

**Word list**
Bark
Bone
Fetch
Leash
Nose
Paws
Puppy
Walk

W Y P P U P
L E A S H A
G B W A L K
N O S E S R
T N A I L A
F E T C H B

Answers on page 269

# Up Front

Put a letter in the blank space on each line to make a word that fits the clue in parentheses. Then read down to answer this riddle: What game do cows like to play?

M̲IDDLE        (center)
O̲MELET        (egg breakfast)
O̲CTOPUS        (eight-armed creature)
S̲ILLY        (foolish)
I̲CING        (cake frosting)
C̲AVE        (underground home)
A̲LMOST        (nearly)
__ITTLE        (small)
__ARROT        (orange veggie)
__APPY        (glad)
__MBULANCE        (emergency vehicle)
__GLOO        (ice house)
__OAR        (make a sound like a lion)
__TAND        (get up)

Answers on page 269

# Special Day

Put each word below into the grid in alphabetical order from A to I. Then read down the starred column to find the name of a special day.

FLOWER

GEESE

CALL

ENJOY

BARK

HOME

ASHES

INK

DEAL

# Letter Moving

Follow the directions below to spell the first part
of a nursery rhyme.

Write the letter A into spaces 8, 18, and 22.
Write the letter C into spaces 9 and 23.
Write the letter E into spaces 6, 15, and 27.
Write the letter H into space 11.
Write the letter I into spaces 2 and 20.
Write the letter J into space 7.
Write the letter K into space 10.
Write the letter L into spaces 1 and 5.
Write the letter N into spaces 14, 21, and 26.
Write the letter O into spaces 12 and 24.
Write the letter R into spaces 13, 16, 25, and 28.
Write the letter S into space 17.
Write the letter T into spaces 3, 4, and 19.

| L | I | T | T | L | e | | J | A | C | K |
|---|---|---|---|---|---|---|---|---|---|---|
| 1 | 2 | 3 | 4 | 5 | 6 | | 7 | 8 | 9 | 10 |

| h | O | r | n | e | r | | S | A | T | |
|---|---|---|---|---|---|---|---|---|---|---|
| 11 | 12 | 13 | 14 | 15 | 16 | | 17 | 18 | 19 | |

| I | n | | A | | C | O | r | n | e | r |
|---|---|---|---|---|---|---|---|---|---|---|
| 20 | 21 | | 22 | | 23 | 24 | 25 | 26 | 27 | 28 |

Answer on page 269

# Volcano Maze

Help the scientist get down the mountain to his escape helicopter without crossing the lava flow.

Answer on page 269

# Colorful Puddles

Change one letter in each word to make the name of a color. Write the color names on the lines, and then color each puddle of paint to match.

1. glue

*blue*

2. rod

*red*

3. greet

*green*

4. fellow
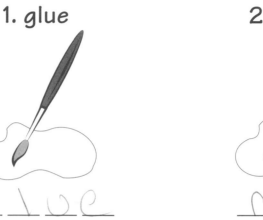
*yellow*

5. crown

_____

6. whine

*white*

7. block
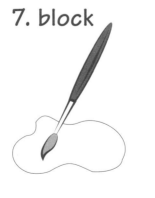
_____

8. link

*Pink*

9. grab

_____

Answers on page 270

# Desserts Crisscross

Place the dessert choices listed below into the diagram so that they interlock as in a crossword. Use each word only once. Ignore the space in *ICE CREAM*, and enter it as *ICECREAM*.

**3 Letters**
Pie

**4 Letters**
Cake

**5 Letters**
Crepe
Fruit

**6 Letters**
Cookie
Eclair
Mousse
Sundae

**7 Letters**
Cupcake
Custard
Pudding

**8 Letters**
Doughnut
Ice Cream

Answers on page 270

# Car Fun

Fill in the missing letters to make words that have *car* in them.

1. a large wagon — car ___
2. may be taped to a gift — car ___
3. keeps your neck warm — ___ car ___
4. to hold and take somewhere — car ___ ___
5. to frighten — ___ car ___
6. to shape with a knife — car ___ ___
7. a vegetable — car ___ ___ ___
8. a funny drawing — car ___ ___ ___ ___
9. a fish — car ___
10. a layer of fabric that covers the floor — car ___ ___ ___
11. a box for shipping things — car ___ ___ ___
12. someone who builds with wood — car ___ ___ ___ ___ ___ ___

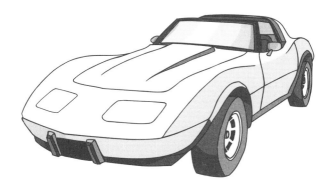

Answers on page 270

# Ooooh!

All 14 words on the list end with an "oo" sound and are hidden in the grid below. Look across and down for them. Circle each word as you find it, and cross it off the list. We found *Flew* for you.

**Word list**

Chew
~~Flew~~
~~Grew~~
Igloo
Moo
Shampoo
Shoe
Threw
Through
Tutu
View
Who
Yahoo
Zoo

Answers on page 270

# A Special Gift

Look at the circled words in each sentence. Figure out which letter is in the first two words but not in the third word. Write the letter in the box. When you are done, read the letters in order to find out what toy is in the gift box.

1. ☐ It's in (first) and (second) but not in (third.)

2. ☐ It's in (hawk) and (goat) but not in (deer.)

3. ☐ It's in (dime) and (nickel) but not in (penny.)

4. ☐ It's in (hill) and (lake) but not in (river.)

5. ☐ It's in (blue) and (brown) but not in (red.)

6. ☐ It's in (cool) and (hot) but not in (warm.)

7. ☐ It's in (sand) and (crab) but not in (shell.)

8. ☐ It's in (kite) and (top) but not in (ball.)

Draw what you think the toy looks like.

Answers on page 270

# Look a Round

Something round is hidden between two or more words in every sentence below. Circle each word as you find it, and cross it off the list. (Don't pay attention to punctuation.) Be aware: Sentence 9 has two round things in it. To get you started, we found *Wheel* in sentence 1 and crossed it off the list.

**Word list**

Bagel
Button
Halo
Hoop
Letter O
Ring
Softball
Tire
Waist
~~Wheel~~

1. I saw he elbowed his way through the crowd.
2. Today's good, but tonight isn't.
3. "Online I use Yahoo," Peter said.
4. Dancers like soft ballet slippers.
5. I have to wash a load of laundry.
6. Who was your teacher in grade school?
7. In Iowa I stood in a cornfield.
8. Where's the bag Elmo brought?
9. Why can't I read our letter out loud?

Answers on page 270

# People Crisscross

Place the people words listed below into the grid so that they interlock as in a crossword. When you are finished, all the words will have been used exactly once. (Ignore the hyphen in *GROWN-UP*, and enter it as *GROWNUP*.)

**3 Letters**
Boy
Kid
Lad

**4 Letters**
Girl
Lady
Lass

**5 Letters**
Adult
Child
Woman

**6 Letters**
Infant
Person

**7 Letters**
Grown-up
Toddler

**8 Letters**
Teenager

**9 Letters**
Gentleman

Answers on page 270

# Website

Help the little bug cross the spiderwebs
to avoid the spiders.

START

FINISH

Answer on page 270

# C-Ya

The C sound can be soft like an S or hard like a K. Fill in the blanks to these words with either a C, S, or K. The pictures are clues to what the words are.

1. F A C E

2. S U N

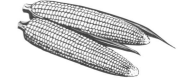

3. C O R N

4. B O O K

5. C H U R C H

6. C L O C K

7. C H I C K E N

Answers on page 270

# Look for These Cs

Now that you know what a C can sound like, find things in this picture that start with the letter C. Finding 20 would be COOL. Finding 25 would be COMPLETELY amazing!

Answers on page 270

# Flight Plan

All the words in the word list are things that fly. Find the words in the grid, which is shaped like a kite with a tail. Look across, down, and diagonally from left to right. Circle each word as you find it, and cross it off the word list.

**Word list**

Bat
Blimp
Butterfly
Dart
Eagle
Finch
Flea
Frisbee
Hawk
Jet
Kite
Pigeon
Plane
Spear
Superman
UFO

```
                    S
                 M  P  P
              D  S  O  L  E
           K  A  U  F  O  A  A
        S  I  R  P  Q  F  G  N  R
     B  U  T  T  E  R  F  L  Y  E  U
        J  E  T  R  I  R  E  E  T
        B  L  I  M  P  I  O  R  A
        A  O  A  I  S  C  K
           T  N  G  B  E
           F  T  E  E  S
              I  O  E
                 N
                 C
                    H
                       A
                          W
                             K
```

Answers on page 270

# Paint a Picture

Find a hidden picture in this grid by coloring in the correct squares in each row. For example, in Row 1, color in the squares C, D, E, and F. When you're done, you'll find something outstanding.

Row 1 C, D, E, F

Row 2 B, C, D, E, F

Row 3 A, B, E, F

Row 4 D, E

Row 5 C, D

Row 6 B, C, G, H, I, J, K

Row 7 A, B, E, F, G, H, I, J, K, L, M

Row 8 A, B, C, D, E, F, G, H, I, J, K, L, M, N, O

Row 9 A, B, C, D, E, F, G, H, I, J, K, L, M, N, O, P

Row 10 B, C, D, E, F, G, H, I, J, K, L, M, N, O

Row 11 D, E, F, G, H, I, J, K, L, M

Row 12 F, I

Row 13 G, J

Row 14 H, K

Row 15 C, D, E, F, G, H, I, J

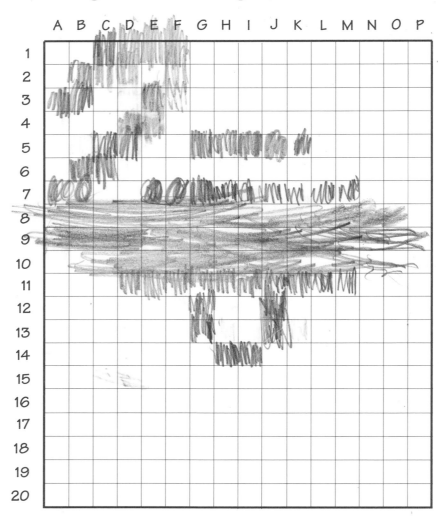

Row 16 C, H

Row 17 H

Row 18 H

Row 19 H

Row 20 F, G, H

Answer on page 270

# Blended Crisscrosses

The words that go into the two crisscrosses have been listed together on the left. One crisscross contains BUGS, and the other contains CLEANING SUPPLIES. Using the letters that are already there, fill in the grid with the correct words. Cross out each word after you place it.

**3 Letters**
Bee
Fly
Mop

**4 Letters**
Flea
Gnat
Moth
Soap

**5 Letters**
Broom
Brush
Towel

**6 Letters**
Bedbug
Bleach
Bucket
Hornet

**7 Letters**
Termite

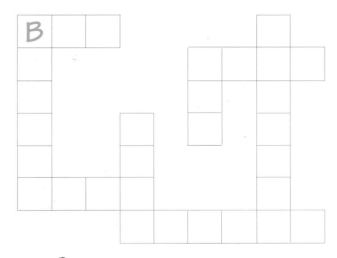

Answers on page 271

# Animal Maker

Replace one letter of each word to make an animal word.

1. cab      _____cat_____

2. dig      _____

3. boat      _____

4. pin      _____

5. dunk      _____

6. bet      _____

7. snare      _____

8. share      _____

9. grab      _____

10. for      _____

11. beam      _____

12. and      _____

13. seat      _____

14. bed      _____

15. while      _____

16. slam      _____

17. deed      _____

18. flu      _____

19. oil      _____

20. carrot      _____

21. gel      _____

22. from      _____

23. beater      _____

24. cloth      _____

25. swam      _____

26. road      _____

27. work      _____

28. store      _____

Answers on page 271

# Stargazing

See if you can find the only path through this stellar maze.
We bet you'll be seeing stars before you're done
with this puzzle!

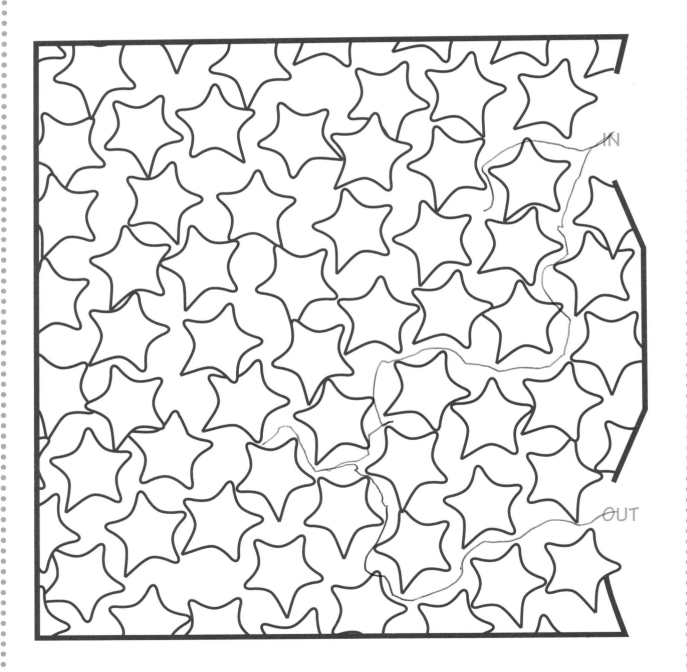

Answer on page 271

# ABC Code

Change each letter below to the one that comes before it in the alphabet to find three riddles and answers. Here's the alphabet to help you along.

A B C D E F G H I J K L M N O P Q R S T U V W X Y Z

1. XIBU  LJOE  PG  CJSUIEBZ  EJE

   *WHAT*
   _____

   UIF  GSPH  IBWF?  B  IPQQZ  POF.
   _____

2. XIZ  EPFT  B  EPH  XBH  JUT  UBJM?
   _____

   CFDBVTF  OP  POF  XJMM  XBH  JU
   _____

   GPS  IJN.
   _____

3. XIBU  EP  ZPV  DBMM  B  DPX
   _____

   FBUJOH  HSBTT?  B  MBXO  NPP-FS.
   _____

Answers on page 271

# Another True or False

Read each sentence. If it's true, circle the letter in the True column. If it's false, circle the letter in the False column. Then read the circled letters from top to bottom to find the name of a vegetable.

|  | True | False |
|---|---|---|
| A quarter is worth 25 cents. | S | C |
| A triangle has four sides. | A | P |
| An orange is a fruit. | I | B |
| Hawaii is a U.S. state. | N | B |
| 3 - 1 = 1 | E | A |
| Italy is in Europe. | C | G |
| July is in winter. | E | H |

# Too Much

Each pair of words will be related to each other if you cross out just one extra letter in each word. (The letter can be at the beginning, the middle, or the end of the word.) You do not have to change the order of any of the letters. The categories at the top of each list provide clues about the pair of words you're looking for. Example: Cross out the H in HARMS to make ARMS.

*Parts of the Body*

Harms

Flingers

*Vegetables*

Peals

Corny

*Birds*

Crown

Beagle

*Bodies of Water*

Flake

Pound

*Planets*

Hearth

Mares

*Farm Animals*

Hoarse

Ping

*Meats*

Streak

Beacon

*Numbers*

Thirsty

Weighty

*Musical Instruments*

Thorn

Sharp

*Desserts*

Nice Scream

Dapple Pine

Answers on page 271

# Sun Fun

Write the compound words that match the clues. Each answer contains the word *sun*.

1. The time in the morning when the sun appears above the horizon

   ___ ___ ___ ___ ___ ___ ___

2. The time in the evening when the sun dips below the horizon

   ___ ___ ___ ___ ___ ___ ___

3. Dark glasses that protect the eyes from the sun's glare

   ___ ___ ___ ___ ___ ___ ___ ___ ___ ___

4. A cream or lotion that protects your skin from the sun's rays

   ___ ___ ___ ___ ___ ___ ___ ___ ___

5. The light from the sun

   ___ ___ ___ ___ ___ ___ ___ ___

6. A device that uses the sun's light to show the time

   ___ ___ ___ ___ ___ ___ ___

7. A large flower with yellow petals and a dark center

   ___ ___ ___ ___ ___ ___ ___ ___ ___

8. A browning of the skin caused by being out in the sun

   ___ ___ ___ ___ ___ ___

9. A ray of sunlight

   ___ ___ ___ ___ ___ ___ ___

10. Sore, red skin caused by staying out in the sun too long

    ___ ___ ___ ___ ___ ___ ___

Answers on page 271

# Mystery Star

Here's a short story about a famous person. To find out who the person is, put only the capitalized words horizontally into the grid below. Use the number of letters in each word and the letters already in the grid as a guide. Then read down the starred column to find the famous person's name.

I am a popular SINGER who was born in KENTWOOD, Louisiana on DECEMBER 2, 1981. As a YOUNG girl I sang in CHURCH choirs. Later on I was a part of The Mickey MOUSE Club. My first album, BABY One More Time, made me a huge success. Some of my other works include the song "OVERPROTECTED" and the album In the Zone, on which my idol, MADONNA, performed with me. I have won many musical AWARDS.

I branched out into other areas by appearing in the movie CROSSROADS, forming a charitable FOUNDATION to help children, and launching a perfume called CURIOUS.

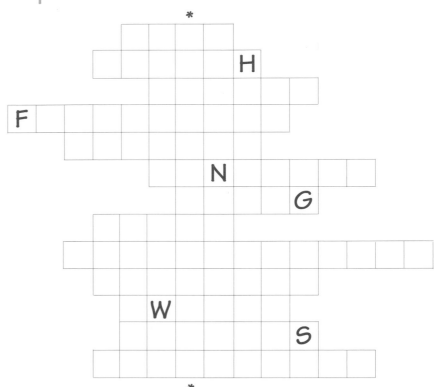

Answers on page 271

# Clothes Lines

All the words in the word list are things that you wear. Find these words in the grid, which is shaped like a shirt. Look across, down, and diagonally. Circle each word as you find it, and cross it off the word list.

**Word list**

Baseball cap
Belt
Coat
Hat
Jeans
Pajamas
Pants
Robe
Shorts
Skirt
Socks
Suit
Sweater
T-shirt
Tank top
Underwear

```
        H T U           R T L
      E B A S E B A L L C A P
      S K I R T S H I R T N O E C
      U P A J A M A S S J K B A L
      I O U U N D E R W E A R S T
      T E J   K R O B E A   A C K
            T E T S A N
            O P A N T S
            P B W E E O
            A T E S R C
            H I R L T K
            S H O R T S
```

Answers on page 271

# Haunted House Maze

You're trapped on the roof of a haunted house, and you have to find your way through the house and out the front door. Watch where you're going. Some rooms and stairs lead to dead ends—or worse!

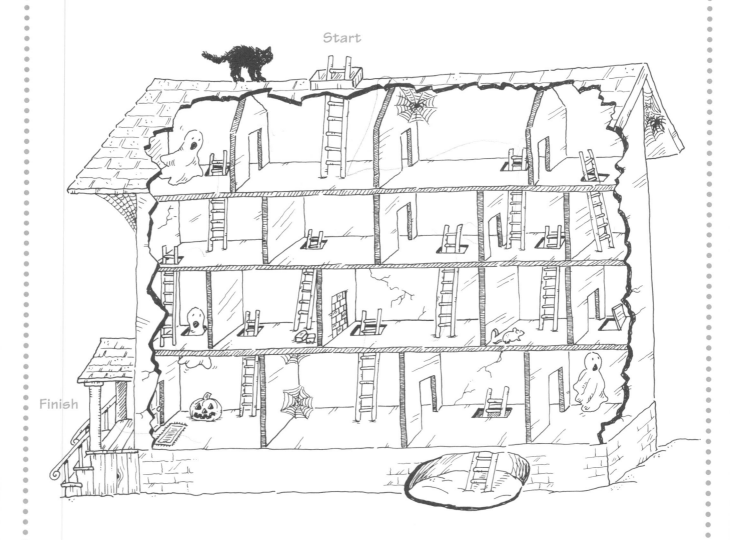

Start

Finish

Answer on page 271

# Triplets

Some letters in the grid below appear three times. Cross those letters out. Put the leftover letters into the spaces below. Go from left to right and top to bottom to answer this riddle: What pets don't mind getting stepped on?

| Z | Z | I | I | D | D | D | Y |
|---|---|---|---|---|---|---|---|
| Z | I | C | L | L | L | Y | Y |
| O | V | V | N | U | U | U | A |
| V | O | Q | N | R | J | J | G |
| Q | K | O | N | M | J | P | G |
| H | K | Q | K | M | M | G | F |
| E | H | H | W | W | T | F | F |
| B | B | B | S | W | X | X | X |

Riddle answer: __ __ __ __ __ __ __

Now, do the same thing here to answer this riddle: What rooms cannot be entered?

| M | K | G | T | T | I |
|---|---|---|---|---|---|
| B | V | Q | T | E | U |
| B | Q | V | K | S | E |
| K | H | B | V | P | E |
| Q | W | J | G | R | P |
| F | P | O | N | I | D |
| W | J | C | N | D | A |
| W | C | G | I | D | O |
| C | N | F | M | L | A |
| L | S | J | L | F | A |

Riddle answer: __ __ __ __ __ __ __ __ __

Answers on page 271

# Going in Circles

In one way or another, these words represent eight things that go in circles. For each circle, begin at one letter, and read the word either clockwise or counterclockwise.

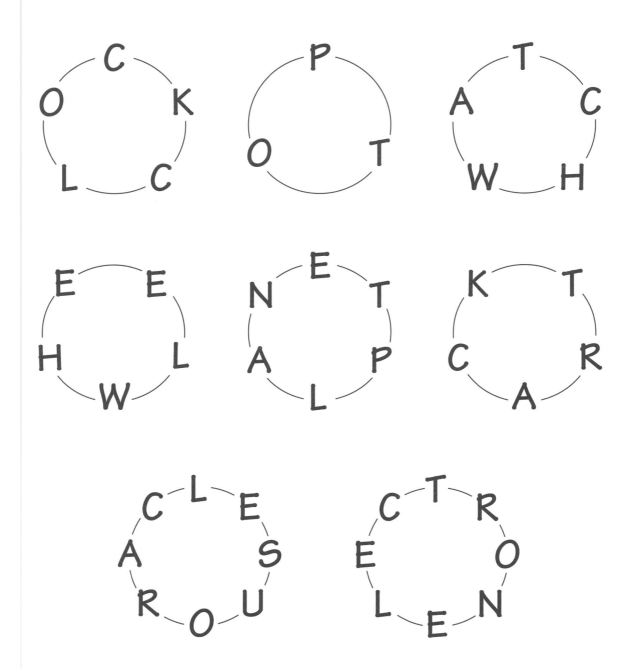

Answers on page 271

# Mix and Match

Rearrange the letters in each word on the left so you can
add it to the word on the right to form a new word.
(This first set is easy, but be prepared!
It will get harder as you move along.)

1. NAP _____CAKE
2. KIN _____STAND
3. NO _____LINE
4. TOP _____BELLY
5. MAD _____AGE

Now try a matching game.
Rearrange the letters in the words next to the numbers
to form a new word with any of the words on the right.

1. MEAT _____DROP
2. ART _____MATE
3. TIP _____MY
4. WED _____GET
5. MUG _____FALL

Now try the matching game in reverse!

1. _____ELF        AM
2. _____KING       BEAR
3. _____DROP       PALS
4. _____STICK      SIT
5. _____FOOT       RATE

Answers on page 271

# Dollars and Cents

Draw a line from the circle next to each amount on the left to the circle next to its matching amount on the right. Write the letters in order on the matching numbered lines to solve the riddle.

2 quarters (1)                    (U) 1 dime

3 dimes (2)                       (R) 1 dollar bill

2 nickels (3)                     (F) 1 half dollar

4 quarters (4)                    (O) 1 quarter, 1 nickel

8 nickels (5)                     (C) 4 dimes

3 quarters (6)                    (S) 8 quarters

7 nickels (7)                     (N) 35 pennies

5 quarters (8)                    (E) 7 dimes 1 nickel

2 dollar bills (9)                (T) 125 pennies

Riddle: What's the difference between an old penny and a new nickel?

Answer to riddle: ___ ___ ___ ___   ___ ___ ___ ___ ___
                               1   2   3   4    5   6   7   8   9

Answers on page 272

# In D

All the words in the word list start with the letter D. Find these words in the grid, which is shaped like a capital D. Look across, up, down, and diagonally. Circle each word as you find it, and cross it off the word list.

**Word list**

Daddy
Daffodil
Daisy
Day
Daylight
Deep
Dessert
Dial
Did
Dinosaur
Dip
Dishwasher
Dives
Dog
Doodle
Dressed
Drum
Dumb

```
D  D  A  D  D  Y  O
D  I  N  O  S  A  U  R
L  S  P  G  H  D  I  I  D
D  H  D        I  S  A  D
A  W  R              A  Y  O
F  A  E              N  L  O
F  S  S              D  I  D
O  H  S              D  G  L
D  E  E        D  W  H  E
I  R  D  E  S  S  E  R  T
L  A  U  D  I  V  E  S
R  D  U  M  B  F  P
```

Answers on page 272

# Add a Word

Each of the following four words can have the same three-letter word added to their beginning to make new words. Find that three-letter word.

_____ get

_____ tune

_____ give

_____ bid

Find another three-letter word to place before these four words.

_____ go

_____ ton

_____ pet

_____ rot

Now here's a hard one to find.

_____ or

_____ age

_____ hunt

_____ date

Answers on page 272

# An Apple a Day

Help this hungry worm make it through the tasty treat.

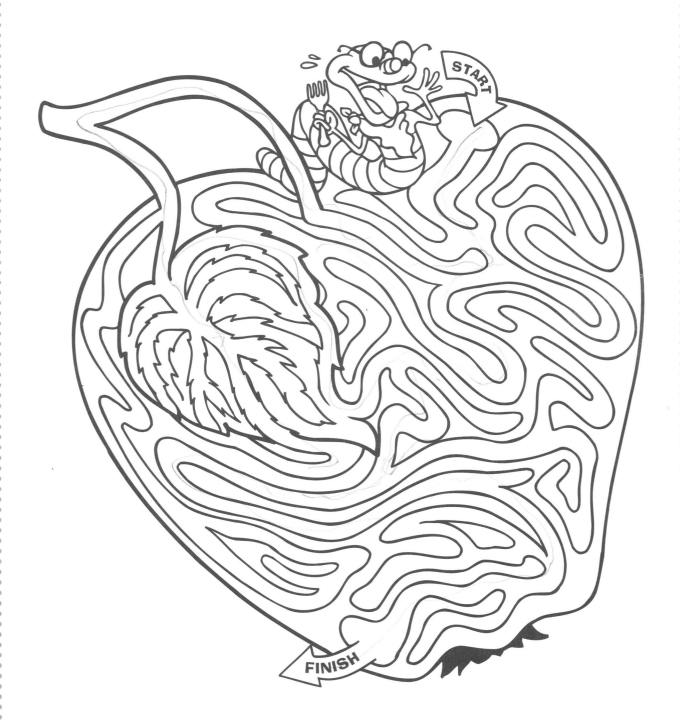

Answer on page 272

# Picture Crossword

Look at the pictures, and name each one. Then write the words in the correct numbered spaces. Be sure to check to see if the word should be written across or down.

Across

Down

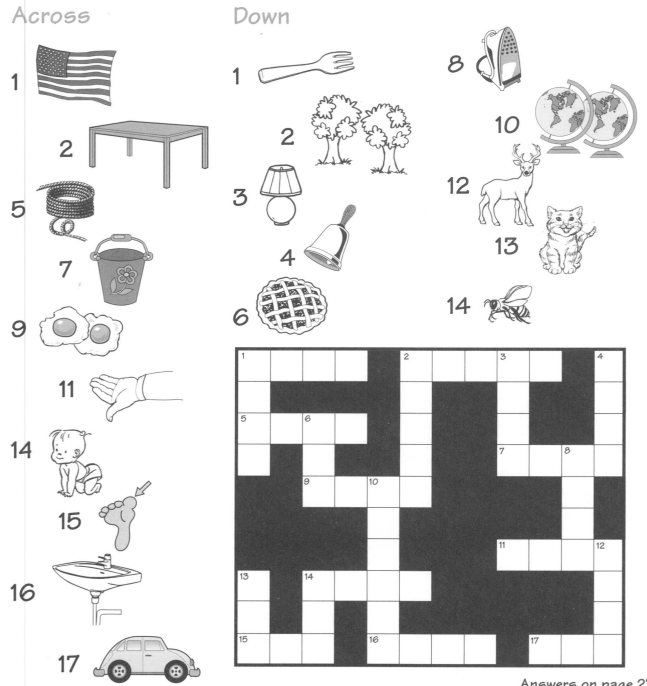

Answers on page 272

# Crack the Code

This "pigpen code" was developed during the Civil War. It gets its name from the grid that looks like a pigpen. Study the code to see how it works, and then use it to find the answer to the riddle at the bottom of the page.

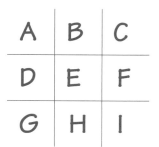

Riddle: What do you call a room with 50 pigs on one side and 50 deer on the other?

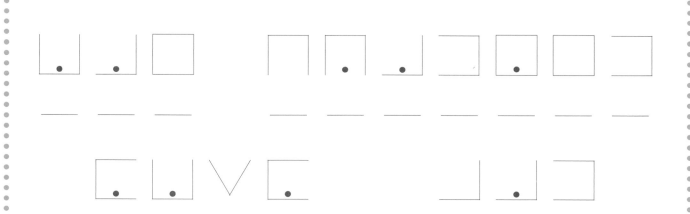

Answer on page 272

# 'Tis the Season

The answers to the clues are words related to seasons or weather. Fill in the blanks, and then write the circled letters on the numbered lines to answer the riddle.

1. The season after fall __ ◯ __ __ __ __

2. A small shallow pool of water left after the rain ◯ __ __ __ __ __

3. Soft flakes of ice ◯ __ __ __

4. A flash of light in the sky __ __ __ __ ◯ __ __ __ __

5. A cloud that is close to the earth's surface __ __ ◯

6. A strong wind with rain __ __ __ ◯ __

7. The season after spring __ __ __ __ ◯ __

8. Moving air __ ◯ __ __

9. A loud rumbling or cracking sound __ __ __ ◯ __ __ __

10. Another name for "fall" __ __ __ __ ◯ __

Riddle: What is a frog's favorite time of year?

Answer: __ __ __ __ __ __ __ __ __ __ __ !

3  2  6  8  9  5  4  1  10  7

Answers on page 272

# Time and Hair

The word *TIME* can be changed into many new words. Change the underlined letters to new letters to make words that answer the clues. We did one for you.

| Word | Clues | New word |
|------|-------|----------|
| <u>T</u>IME | 10 cent coin | DIME |
| T<u>I</u>ME | The opposite of wild | _____ |
| TI<u>ME</u> | On the bathroom floor | _____ |
| TI<u>ME</u> | Really little | _____ |
| <u>T</u>IME | A green fruit | _____ |
| T<u>IME</u> | Grows in the forest | _____ |

This time make HAIR changes.

| Word | Clues | New word |
|------|-------|----------|
| <u>H</u>AIR | Lots of food and fun rides | _____ |
| HA<u>IR</u> | The opposite of soft | _____ |
| HAI<u>R</u> | Falling ice | _____ |
| <u>H</u>AIR | Two together | _____ |
| HA<u>IR</u> | 1/2 | _____ |

Answers on page 272

# Paint a Picture

Find a hidden picture in this grid by coloring in the correct squares in each row. For example, in Row 1, color in the squares C, D, E, and F. When you're done, you'll find something to give you some smooth moves.

Row 1 C, D, E, F

Row 2 B, C, D, E, F, G

Row 3 B, C, D, E, F, G

Row 4 B, C, D, E, F, G

Row 5 B, C, D, E, F, G

Row 6 B, C, D, E, F, G, H

Row 7 B, C, D, E, F, G, H

Row 8 B, C, D, E, F, G, H, I, J

Row 9 B, C, D, E, F, G, H, I, J, K, L, M, N

Row 10 B, C, D, E, F, G, H, I, J, K, L, M, N

Row 11 B, C, D, E, F, G, H, I, J, K, L, M, N

Row 12 C, D, E, H, I, J, K, L, M, N

Row 13 C, D, E, I, J, K, L, M

Row 14 D, I, M

Row 15 All

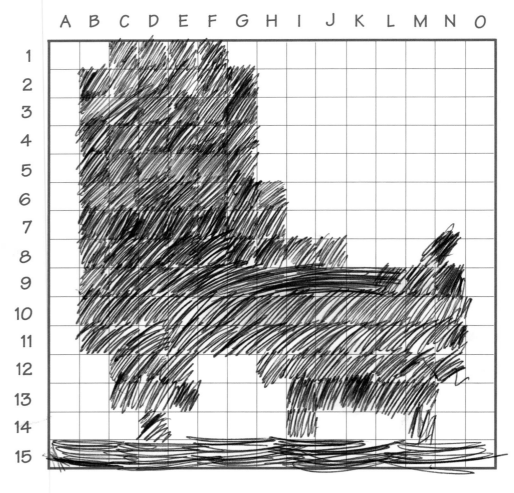

Answer on page 272

# Water Wonders

Riddle: What did the river say to the sea?

To find the answer to the riddle, cross out the following words from the box below.

- Cross out 4 animals that live in water.
- Cross out 4 names of oceans.
- Cross out 4 water sports.
- Cross out 4 kinds of boats.
- Cross out 4 bodies of water.
- Cross out 4 forms of water that fall from the sky.

| IT | LAKE | SEAL | SWIMMING | PACIFIC |
|---|---|---|---|---|
| ROWBOAT | WHALE | FERRY | WAS | RAIN |
| SURFING | SLEET | NICE | ATLANTIC | BAY |
| ARCTIC | SAILBOAT | OCEAN | HAIL | RUNNING |
| GULF | INTO | SCUBA DIVING | OCTOPUS | INDIAN |
| YOU | FISH | TUGBOAT | SNOW | BOATING |

Look at the words that didn't get crossed out. Write them in order on the line below to answer the riddle.

_____

Answer on page 272

# Trivial Quiz

Each question comes with four possible answers.
Circle the correct one.

1. Which of these sport balls is the heaviest?

golf ball          tennis ball          softball          bowling ball

2. If today is Friday the 13th, what day of the month is the 24th?

Monday          Tuesday          Wednesday          Thursday

3. Which of these snack foods starts out as kernels?

potato chips          ice cream          popcorn          licorice

4. From which of these animals do we get wool?

sheep          chimpanzee          caterpillar          fox

5. Which part of your body is impossible to touch with your right hand?

left leg          neck          waist          right elbow

6. Who was the U.S. president right before George W. Bush?

Reagan          Clinton          Lincoln          Kerry

Answers on page 272

# In Outer Space

Help the alien find the hidden words. Start with S, and then go around the path clockwise. Write down every third letter (the first third letter is U) until you have written eight words related to outer space.

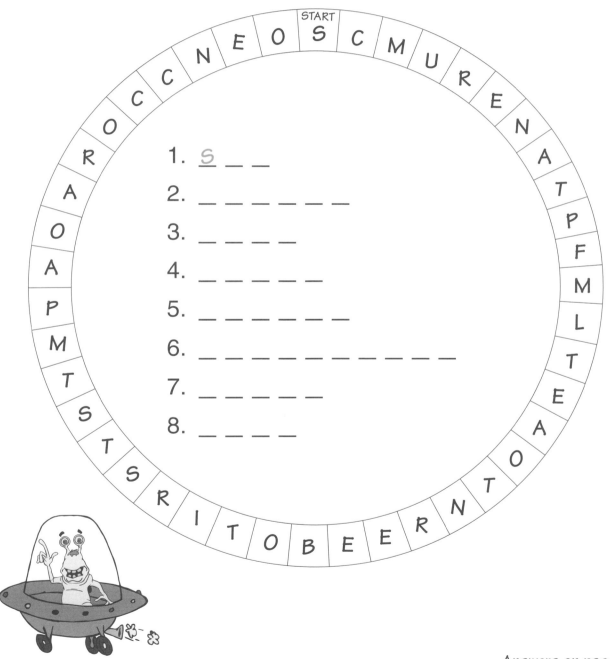

1. S _ _ _
2. _ _ _ _ _ _ _
3. _ _ _ _
4. _ _ _ _ _
5. _ _ _ _ _ _
6. _ _ _ _ _ _ _ _ _
7. _ _ _ _ _ _
8. _ _ _ _

Answers on page 272

# Mystery Musician

Here's a short story about a famous person. To find out who the person is, put only the capitalized words into the grid below. Use the number of letters in each word and the letters already in the grid as a guide. Then read down the starred column to find the famous person's name.

I am a songwriter, musician, and PRODUCER who was born in SAGINAW, Michigan on May 13, 1950. Although I have been BLIND from birth, I learned how to play many musical instruments, including the HARMONICA and PIANO. When I was just THIRTEEN years old I recorded my first major hit, "FINGERTIPS."

Some of my other top songs include "You Are the SUNSHINE of My Life" and "Ebony and IVORY," a DUET which I performed with Paul McCartney. I have won more than 20 Grammy AWARDS. I was inducted into the Rock and Roll Hall of FAME in 1989.

Answers on page 272

# Doubles

Cross out the words that are in both the top and bottom boxes. There will be one extra word in the bottom box. Follow the directions below to find out what to do with that word.

| | | | | |
|---|---|---|---|---|
| HAVE | HOLD | HERE | HIRE | HOPE |
| HOST | HAND | HIVE | HORN | HELP |
| HERS | HEAR | HIDE | HALF | HANG |
| HUGE | HUNT | HOWL | HARP | HARK |
| HYMN | HOSE | HAZE | HAZY | HISS |
| HERD | HOLY | HUMP | HARE | HAIL |

| | | | | | |
|---|---|---|---|---|---|
| HERD | HORN | HANG | HUNT | HOWL | HIRE |
| HAZY | HIDE | HERS | HAND | HAZE | HEAR |
| HUMP | HOLD | HOLY | HYMN | HIVE | HERE |
| HARE | HARK | HOSE | HAVE | HAIL | HOPE |
| HOST | HERO | HELP | HARP | HISS | HALF |
| HUGE | | | | | |

Write the leftover word on this line: _____ hero _____

To find the two meanings of this word, change each letter below to the one that comes before it in the alphabet. Write the new words on the lines.

B  C S B W F   Q F S T P O
a   Brave    per
_____

B  M B S H F   T B O E X J D I
_____

Answers on page 272

# Place Mats

Take a trip around the world right from this page! Just choose one of the three-letter groups, and put it into the blank spaces on each line twice. You'll form the end of one place name and the start of another. You may not know all these places, but you will probably know at least one name on each line. Cross off each letter group as you use it. We did the first one for you.

Letter groups

ANA
AND
ARK
DAM
DEN
IDA
KEN
KEY
LAN
~~ORE~~
PAN
SLO
STA
TON

1. B A L T I M O R E        &        O R E G O N
2. M I ___ ___ ___           &        ___ ___ ___ C A S T E R
3. L O U I S I ___ ___ ___   &        ___ ___ ___ H E I M
4. P R I N C E ___ ___ ___   &        ___ ___ ___ G A
5. T U R ___ ___ ___         &        ___ ___ ___ W E S T
6. F L O R ___ ___ ___       &        ___ ___ ___ H O
7. N E W ___ ___ ___         &        ___ ___ ___ A N S A S
8. C L E V E L ___ ___ ___   &        ___ ___ ___ O V E R
9. D R E S ___ ___ ___       &        ___ ___ ___ V E R
10. A M S T E R ___ ___ ___  &        ___ ___ ___ A S C U S
11. O ___ ___ ___            &        ___ ___ ___ V A K I A
12. J A ___ ___ ___          &        ___ ___ ___ A M A
13. A U G U ___ ___ ___      &        ___ ___ ___ M F O R D
14. H O B O ___ ___ ___      &        ___ ___ ___ T U C K Y

Answers on pages 272–273

# What's in Common?

The 10 words below all have something in common. Yes, they all end in S, and they're all five letters long. But there's something else. What is it?

NAILS

WINGS

MILES

TRAPS

COLDS

PACES

TALES

WEEPS

HOOTS

PEARS

Figured it out? Not yet? Okay, here's a hint. It has to do with switching a letter.

Answers on page 273

# Word Families

Each of these word groups uses the same two letters together. Fill in the blanks to spell words that answer the clues in parentheses.

1.  A L __ __            (In addition)

    __ A L __            (Part of a football game)

    __ __ A L __         (Largest sea creature)

    __ __ __ __ A L      (Any creature)

2.  __ T O __            (What a red light means)

    T O __ __ __         (Feel)

    __ __ __ T O __      (What some shirts are made of)

    __ __ __ __ __ T O   (What french fries are made of)

3.  P I __ __            (Choose)

    __ __ P I __         (Eye part or student)

    __ __ P I __ __      (Office machine)

    __ __ __ P I __ __   (Leaping)

4.  Z E __ __            (Nothing)

    __ __ Z E            (Stare at the stars)

    __ __ __ Z E __      (Thing to press near a door)

    __ __ __ __ Z E __   (Went "Achoo!")

Answers on page 273

# Jordan's Story

Fill in the blanks with words that contain the letters *or*.
You can use the words in the box if you like, but you'll have
to unscramble them first!

Hi, my name is Jordan! I live in
the state of New _____.
Yesterday I went to the department
_____ to buy a gift for
my Uncle Morty. I waited _____
half an hour, but no sales clerk came
to help me. It was so _____
waiting around! Not only that, but
my feet were getting quite _____!

Just when I thought I would
walk out the door, I saw a salesman
standing in the _____
of the room.

"Hey, I'm a customer, but it
seems you're _____
me," I said.

"I'm _____, sir," said the salesman, "but it's my
first day here and I'm a bit nervous."

"I'll _____ you," I said, "if you can get me a great
deal on a gift for my uncle."

"I'll give you up to _____ percent off any item you
buy," said the salesman.

"Great!" I said. I scooped up three T-shirts and two pairs of
_____. Guess what? I paid no _____ than five
dollars for them!

| | |
|---|---|
| rof | _____ |
| mero | _____ |
| srory | _____ |
| Ykro | _____ |
| strohs | _____ |
| roes | _____ |
| resto | _____ |
| ringob | _____ |
| grifoev | _____ |
| creron | _____ |
| tryof | _____ |
| grinigon | _____ |

Answers on page 273

# School Daze

Oops. Someone took a three-letter word out of each school-related word below and put the words into the box below. Can you get good marks by putting each word from the box into one of the empty spaces to complete each school-related word? Cross off each word as you use it.

| | | | |
|---|---|---|---|
| DEN | DIN | ELL | HIS |
| LIB | LIT | MET | MEW |
| PAL | RAM | RAP | TEA |

1. G E O G _ _ _ H Y
2. _ _ _ T O R Y
3. R E A _ _ _ _ G
4. S P _ _ _ I N G
5. A R I T H _ _ _ I C
6. _ _ _ _ C H E R
7. P R I N C I _ _ _ _
8. _ _ _ _ R A R Y
9. S T U _ _ _ _ T
10. G _ _ _ M A R
11. _ _ _ _ E R A T U R E
12. H O _ _ _ O R K

Answers on page 273

# Tricky Tongue Twisters

All the words in each sentence below begin with the same letter. Write the missing letters on the lines. Then try reading each sentence aloud quickly three times. It's a lot harder than it looks!

1. ___even ___nakes ___lithered ___ilently.

2. ___usy ___akers ___usily ___aked ___read.

3. ___eggy ___ainted ___retty ___urple ___arrots.

4. ___innie ___aited ___hile ___arren ___ent ___alking.

5. ___rant ___rows ___reen ___rass.

6. ___ily ___ikes ___icking ___ollipops.

7. ___roy's ___rain ___ooted ___wo ___imes.

8. ___ob ___ows ___owboats ___apidly.

9. ___ed's ___ine ___ewts ___ibbled ___uts.

10. ___our ___ireflies ___lew ___rom ___rance.

Answers on page 273

# Outer Space Word Search

Liftoff! Find and circle the 11 space-related words from the word list. Look forward or backward, up or down, and diagonally, and cross each word off as you find it.

Word list

| | | |
|---|---|---|
| Astronaut | Mercury | Planet |
| Big Dipper | Meteor | Pluto |
| Earth | Moon | Star |
| | Orbit | Sun |

```
A  S  T  R  O  N  A  U  T  P  R  O
N  O  O  M  M  N  U  S  R  O  M  E
M  E  T  E  O  R  M  T  O  T  E  A
O  L  S  U  V  W  I  E  I  U  R  R
S  L  T  U  T  C  L  N  N  L  C  T
G  R  E  I  R  L  M  A  N  P  U  H
D  R  B  E  A  A  S  L  A  R  R  E
S  R  A  I  T  A  P  P  L  M  Y  W
O  S  U  M  S  R  Q  P  D  G  I  K
B  I  G  D  I  P  P  E  R  L  Y  S
```

Answers on page 273

# Up Front

Make words by filling in the blanks with pronouns. Pronouns are words that stand for nouns, such as *he, she, us,* and *them.* You may use a pronoun more than once.

1. __ __ B

2. B __ __ __

3. NA __ __

4. __ __ AD

5. C __ __ __ RY

6. C __ __ __ NEY

7. DI __ __ __ S

8. W __ __ H

9. AN __ __ __ __

10. __ __ ATHER

11. __ __ LT

12. K __ __ E

13. __ __ E

14. S __ __ LL

15. W __ __ __ PER

16. A __ __

17. T __ __ __ BLE

18. C __ __ ST

19. TEAC __ __ __

20. __ __ __ TORY

21. JE __ __ L

22. CA __ __ L

23. __ __ __ TH

24. L __ __ TLE

25. __ __ LP

26. CR __ __ T

27. __ __ __ NG

28. C __ __ __ E

29. WA __ __ __ R

30. W __ __ __ KER

| | |
|---|---|
| he | she |
| her | them |
| him | us |
| it | we |
| me | you |
| his | |

Answers on page 273

# Eliminations

Cross off all the words described in the box.
Then read only the leftover words from top to bottom to
find the answer to this riddle: What is the best spot on
earth to see things?

Cross off:

4 U.S. cities
2 things that you eat with a spoon
3 articles of clothing
3 things to read
3 flowers
3 days of the week
3 boys' names
3 words that rhyme with "hope"

| | | | |
|---|---|---|---|
| MIAMI | DAISY | ON | JOE |
| PUDDING | jeans | BOOK | TUESDAY |
| AN | | ROSE | SHIRT |
| NEWSPAPER | CLEVELAND | | |
| NOPE | Philadelphia | FRIDAY | |
| | | EYE | MENU |
| GEORGE | DRESS | | |
| MONDAY | PHOENIX | HENRY | TULIP |
| MOPE | SOUP | LAND | ROPE |

Answer on page 273

# Scrambled Sports

Use the clues to help you figure out the first two words in each puzzle. Then rearrange the letters of your answers to spell the name of a sport.

1. opposite of out          __ __
   a place for eggs          __ __ __ __
   a sport that requires a ball and racket          __ __ __ __ __ __ __

2. another name for autumn          __ __ __ __
   a tall shoe          __ __ __ __
   a sport played with an oval ball          __ __ __ __ __ __ __ __

3. a form of "to be"          __ __
   a male ruler          __ __ __ __
   a sport in which people glide over snow          __ __ __ __ __ __

4. a room for scientific experiments          __ __ __
   large bundles of hay          __ __ __ __
   a sport that is played with
   a ball and a bat          __ __ __ __ __ __ __ __

5. a loud noise or explosion          __ __ __ __ __
   cold, empty, and depressing          __ __ __ __ __
   a sport in which players throw
   a ball through a hoop          __ __ __ __ __ __ __ __ __ __

Answers on page 273

# Find the Football

Each sentence below contains a hidden word or phrase relating to football. Find each football word, and underline it. We did the first one for you.

1. Do I get a <u>quarter back</u> in change from my dollar?

2. It was the first downpour of the rainy season.

3. Tampa's stadium gets very full on Sundays.

4. The secretary had to stack letters for her boss.

5. Ethel met Lucy at the TV studio.

6. The spider spun terrible webs.

7. The angry boy pulled the second hand off of the watch.

8. Finding the computer room open, Al typed up the list.

9. Is that clover Tim eats for a snack?

10. Sue's house is as big a mess as you'll ever see.

Answers on page 273

# Hidden Animals

The name of an animal is hidden in each sentence below. Underline the names, and write them on the lines. The first one has been done for you.

1. Don't forget to <u>do good</u> every day.  d o g
2. The wheel on the cart looks broken.  ___ ___ ___
3. The lab at the end of the street is closed.  ___ ___ ___
4. This is not a common key because it has been cast in gold.  ___ ___ ___ ___ ___ ___
5. Philip ignores our pleas to eat healthier foods.  ___ ___ ___
6. "America the Beautiful" is a lovely song.  ___ ___ ___
7. Are you going to address all those envelopes?  ___ ___ ___
8. Ali only likes vegetables that are cooked.  ___ ___ ___ ___
9. The sea gleams at sunset.  ___ ___ ___ ___ ___
10. The boy made eraser marks on the paper.  ___ ___ ___ ___
11. If lying down hurts your back, stand up and stretch.  ___ ___ ___

Riddle Time! Unscramble the circled letters above, and write them on the lines below to find the answer.

Riddle: How do camels hide in the desert?

Answer: They use ___ ___ ___ ___ ___ - ___ ___ ___ ___ ___ !

Answers on page 273

# Anthill

Help these worker ants get food to their queen. Watch out for the ants blocking the tunnels!

Answer on page 273

# What a Year!

One year on Earth is about 365 days. One year on Mercury, the closest planet to the Sun, takes only 88 Earth-days! Suppose a person were 5 years old on Earth. How old would that person be on Mercury? To find out, first unscramble the words below and then write them on the lines. Each word relates to the passing of time. Then write the circled letters in order at the bottom of the page to find the answer.

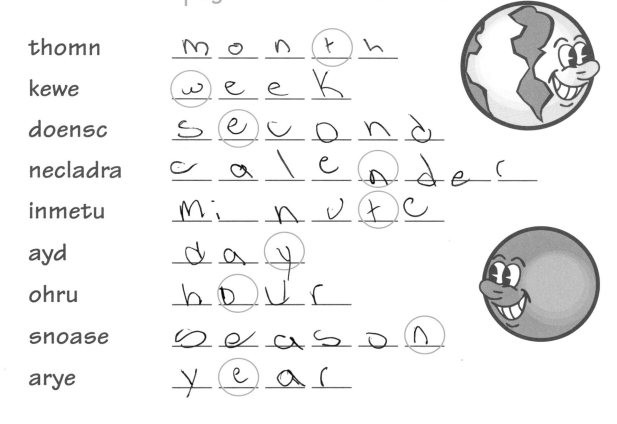

thomn    M o n t h

kewe    w e e k

doensc    s e c o n d

necladra    c a l e n d e r

inmetu    M i n u t e

ayd    d a y

ohru    h o u r

snoase    s e a s o n

arye    y e a r

A five-year old would be about

t w e n t y - o n e

years old on Mercury.

Answers on page 274

# Famous Tales and Rhymes

Use the letters above the diagrams only once to fill in the empty squares. The word across is the first word of a fairy tale or nursery rhyme, and the word down is its second word. The letter at the intersection is part of both words.

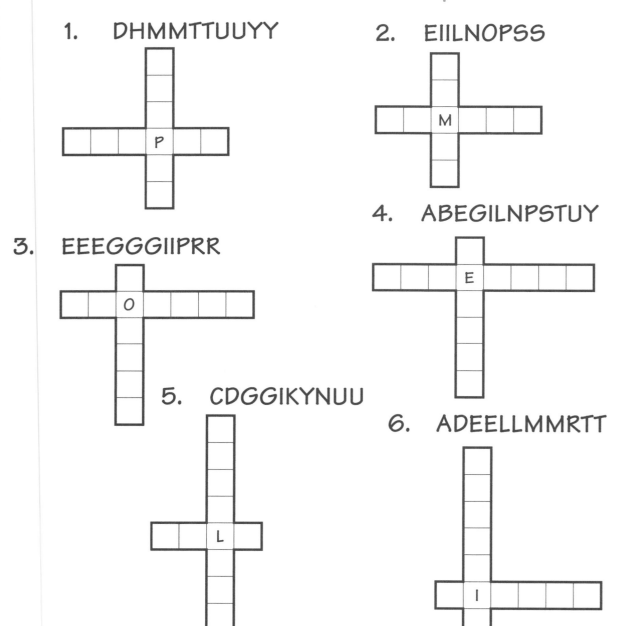

1. DHMMTTUUYY

2. EIILNOPSS

3. EEEGGGIIPRR

4. ABEGILNPSTUY

5. CDGGIKYNUU

6. ADEELLMMRTT

Answers on page 274

# Around the House

The words on the roof are all things you'll see at home.
Find and circle the words in the puzzle.
The words go up, down, across, and diagonally.

| | | | |
|---|---|---|---|
| Bed | Dresser | Radio | Stove |
| Blanket | Fork | Refrigerator | Table |
| Chair | Lamp | Shelf | Telephone |
| Clock | Mirror | Sink | Television |
| Cup | Pillow | Soap | Towel |
| Curtain | Plate | Sofa | Vase |
| Door | Pot | Spoon | Window |

```
C  W  I  N  D  O  W  C  U  C  H  A  I  R  A
U  C  L  K  O  F  L  A  N  L  A  M  T  E  L
R  S  A  P  O  O  N  D  S  O  F  S  O  F  D
T  O  M  I  R  R  O  R  W  C  U  P  R  R  O
A  V  P  L  A  T  M  E  I  K  D  O  E  I  S
I  S  A  C  H  A  I  S  P  O  O  N  F  G  B
N  T  T  S  B  A  R  S  T  E  L  E  K  E  P
R  O  E  M  E  L  R  E  O  N  S  R  M  R  T
P  P  L  A  T  E  A  R  W  Z  O  T  V  A  S
A  B  E  D  E  K  P  N  E  F  F  O  E  T  D
U  R  V  V  N  H  L  E  K  O  A  V  A  O  N
S  A  I  I  S  S  O  A  P  E  N  E  T  R  U
T  D  S  R  H  X  I  C  J  R  T  R  O  L  A
O  I  I  T  E  L  E  P  H  O  N  E  W  A  M
V  O  O  C  L  T  A  B  L  E  M  S  E  O  T
E  K  N  B  F  S  H  E  L  P  I  L  L  O  W
```

Answers on page 274

# Word Magic

Change *cat* to *rug*. Change only one letter at a time. Use the picture clues to help you.

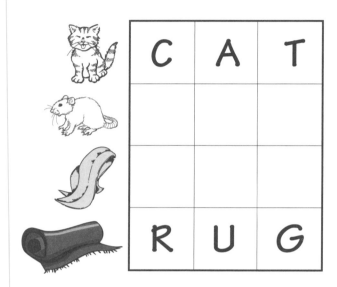

| C | A | T |
|---|---|---|
|   |   |   |
|   |   |   |
| R | U | G |

Now change *sun* to *bed*.

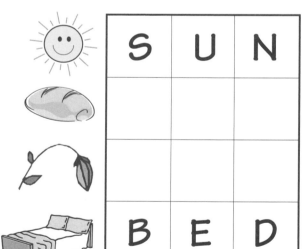

| S | U | N |
|---|---|---|
|   |   |   |
|   |   |   |
| B | E | D |

Now change *leg* to *doe*.

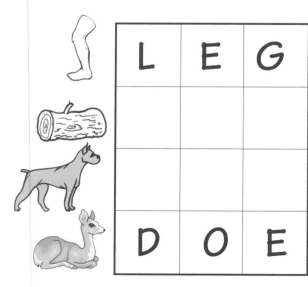

| L | E | G |
|---|---|---|
|   |   |   |
|   |   |   |
| D | O | E |

Answers on page 274

# Bowling Blunders

Can you find 12 or more errors in this bowling scene?

Answers on page 274

# Pinball Panic

Send the ball through the game to get to the high score.

Answer on page 274

# "C" First Americans

All the names in the list are the names of Native American nations that begin with the letter C. Place each name into the grid.

4 Letters
Cree
Crow

5 Letters
Creek

7 Letters
Catawba
Choctaw
Chumash

8 Letters
Cherokee
Cheyenne
Chicasaw
Chippewa
Comanche

9 Letters
Chipewyan

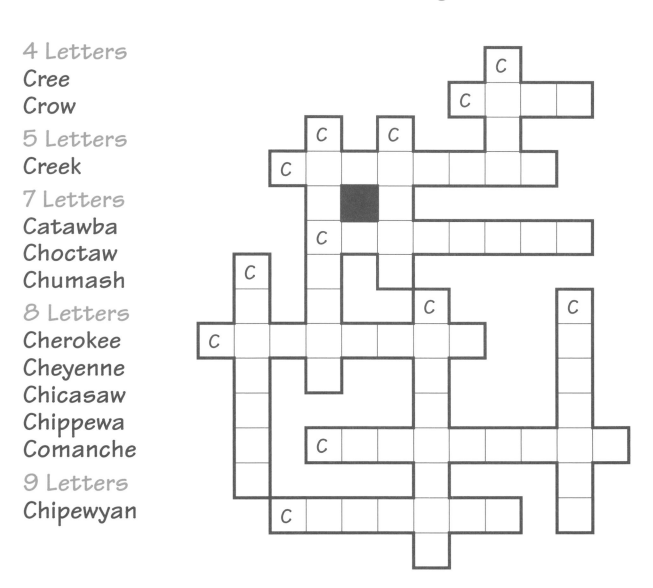

Answers on page 274

# Eliminations

Cross off all the words that are described in the box. Then read only the leftover words from bottom to top to find the riddle to this answer:

Because they "weed" a lot.

| Cross off: | 3 words that rhyme with "sing" |
| 3 family members | 4 girls names |
| 2 names of oceans | 5 colors |
| 4 things you wear on your feet | 2 cities in Europe |

Mother · RING · SMART · Slippers

SISTER · ATLANTIC · LONDON · PURPLE

BLUE · BOOTS · WING · Brother

KING · SO · SOCKS · BARBARA

JANE · Wendy · Farmers · RED

ARE · PACIFIC · Green · ROME

YELLOW · JILL · WHY · Sandals

Answer on page 274

# Recipe for Fun

Fill in the blank space on each line to spell a food item that can be used in baking cookies. Then read down the shaded column to answer this riddle.

**Why did the cookie go to the doctor?**

C _H_ ocolate

Butt _e_ r

_F_ ruit

Cr _e_ am

Fl _L_ our

Oa _t_ meal

Co _c_ onut

_R_ aisins

N _u_ ts

Ja _m_

Le _m_ on

Hone _y_

Answer: _She felt crummy_

She feelt crummy

Answer on page 274

# Paint a Picture

Find a hidden picture in the grid below by coloring in the correct squares in each row. For example, in Row 1, color in the squares D, E, F, G, H, and I. When you're done, you'll find something that could lead to a sticky situation.

Row 1    D, E, F, G, H, I
Row 2    C, D, E, F, G, H, I, J
Row 3    B, C, D, E, F, G, H, I, J, K
Row 4    A, B, C, D, E, F, G, H, I, J, K
Row 5    A, B, C, D, H, I, J, K
Row 6    A, B, C, I, J
Row 7    A, B, C, I, J, Q
Row 8    A, B, C, I, J, P, Q
Row 9    A, B, C, D, H, I, J, K, O, P, Q
Row 10   A, B, C, D, E, F, G, H, I, J, K, L, M, N, O, P
Row 11   A, B, C, D, E, F, G, H, I, J, K, L, M, N, O
Row 12   B, C, D, E, F, G, H, I, J, K, L, M, N
Row 13   C, D, E, F, G, H, I, J, K, L, M

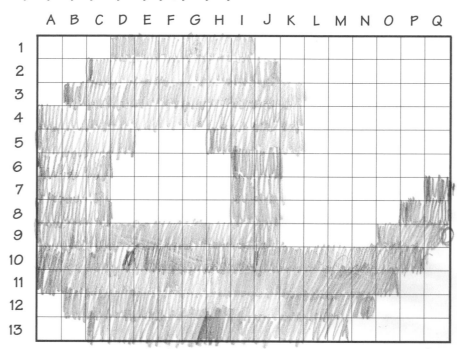

Answer on page 274

# It's in the Cards

Circle the 15 words and phrases about cards and card games hidden in this diamond-shape grid. Words may run forward or backward, up or down, or along diagonals, but they will always be in a straight line.

## Word list

Aces
Clubs
Crazy eights
Deck
Diamonds
Gin
Hearts
Jacks
King
Old maid
Poker
Queen
Solitaire
Spades
War

```
                              G
                          H   O   C
                      F   S   E   R   W
                  O   L   D   M   A   I   D
              S   I   S   N   R   Z   R   H   A
          N   R   E   K   O   P   Y   D   T   P   I
      S   B   U   L   C   M   D   E   C   K   S   N   S
          K   E   R   I   A   T   I   L   O   S   E
              C   O   K   I   N   G   I   N   D
                  A   C   D   E   H   H   A
                      J   L   E   T   P
                          E   U   S
                              Q
```

Answers on page 274

# Famous Cities and Countries

Use the letters above the diagrams only once to fill in the empty squares. The word across is the first word of a city, and the word down is the country where the city is located. The letter in the center square is part of both words.

1. AACEFINPS

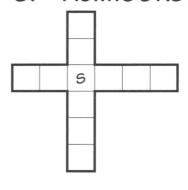

2. AAACDOOORTT

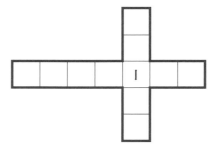

3. ACIMOORSUW

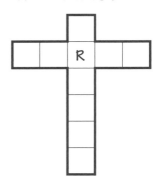

4. ABCEGHIJNN

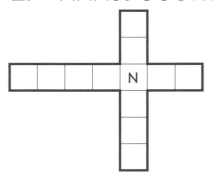

5. ACEIMNNOUX

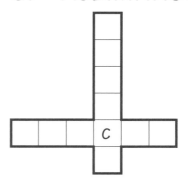

6. EEEIJLLMRRSSU

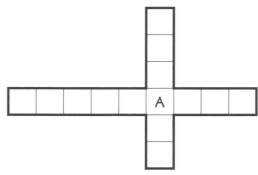

Answers on page 274

# Where's the Wood?

Find each type of wood listed here in one of the sentences below. Look between two or more words, and underline each one as you find it. We found the first one for you and crossed it off the list.

~~ash~~         locust

cedar         maple

ebony         oak

fir            olive

hazel         palm

linden         pine

1. Where w<u>as h</u>e going?
2. Here's the violin Dennis bought.
3. I can make it if I rush.
4. I'm a pleasant person.
5. Let's go to a kite store.
6. She didn't like the bony fish.
7. The store president said, "Hello customers."
8. They wanted to live in Alaska.
9. This is the cap I need.
10. We'll play outside when the haze lifts.
11. The principal made a speech.
12. She placed a rose on the chair.

Answers on page 274

# F Is for Finding

How many things can you find that start with the letter F?
Finding 30 would be FINE.
Finding 40 or more would be FANTASTIC!

Answers on pages 274—275

# End of the Line

Write the correct letter in the blank to spell words that
answer the clues in parentheses.
Then read down to answer this riddle:
### What superhero works at a supermarket?

QUEBE__          (a province in Canada)

PENCI__          (writing tool)

NIGHTMAR__       (frightening dream)

FEVE__           (high body temperature)

STIC__           (long thin piece of wood)


SHAR__           (saltwater fish)

JUDG__           (important person in a courtroom)

MARATHO__        (long race)

QUARTE__         (group of four persons or things)

Answer: _____

Answers on page 275

# Shh!

Place the words about sleeping into the diagram.
Hint: Start with the nine-letter word.
(Ignore any spaces between the words;
for example, enter CONK OUT as CONKOUT.)

**4 Letters**
✓ Dark
✓ Rest

**5 Letters**
✓ Awake
✓ Dream
✓ Quiet
✓ Snore

**6 Letters**
✓ Asleep
✓ Pillow
✓ Sheets
✓ Snooze

**7 Letters**
✓ Bedroom
✓ Blanket
✓ Conk out
✓ Lie down

**8 Letters**
✓ Mattress
✓ Take a nap

**9 Letters**
✓ Nightmare

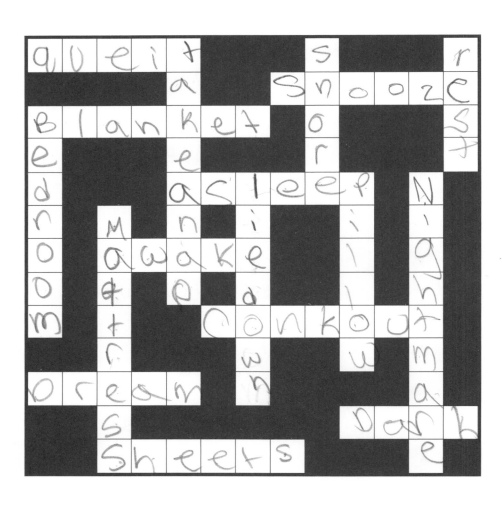

Answers on page 275

# Scrambled Opposites

On each line there are two words that are the opposite
of each other. Unscramble each word. Then write
the pairs of opposites on the lines.
The first one is done for you.

1. RONFT and ABCK        *FRONT and BACK*

2. HHGI and OLW          _____

3. INKD and RULEC        _____

4. UGHLA and RYC         _____

5. SLEO and DINF         _____

6. UDLO and FOST         _____

7. ATEN and SYMSE        _____

8. EVREN and SWALAY      _____

9. ESIAR and REWOL       _____

10. CHIR and OPOR        _____

11. EVSA and PDENS       _____

12. TRTAS and INSHIF     _____

13. RUTE and LASEF       _____

14. KEWA and RONGTS      _____

15. DLWI and META        _____

Answers on page 275

# Shared Words

Each word in the box will form the end of one word and the beginning of another word. Cross off each word in the box as you place them on the blanks.

Example:   M A S *C O T*  &  *C O T* T O N

| AGE | AIR | ANT |
|-----|-----|-----|
| ART | BET | CAN |
| DEN | ERA | HER |
| KIN | ~~ROT~~ | ~~TAR~~ |

1. G U I *t a r*                &   *t a r* G E T
2. P A R *c o t*                &   *R o t* T E N
3. A L P H A *D e t*            &   *b e t* T E R
4. N A P _ _ _ _                &   _ _ _ _ D N E S S
5. P E L I _ _ _                &   _ _ _ D L E
6. O P _ _ _ _                  &   _ _ _ S E R
7. S U D _ _ _ _                &   _ _ _ _ T I S T
8. L U G G _ _ _ _              &   _ _ _ N T
9. B R O T _ _ _ _              &   _ _ _ _ M I T
10. R E P _ _ _ _               &   _ _ _ _ P O R T
11. I N F _ _ _ _               &   _ _ _ _ E L O P E
12. D E P _ _ _ _               &   _ _ _ _ I C L E

Answers on page 275

# Alphabet Soup

Fill in the blanks with one of the 26 letters of the alphabet so that a six-letter word is made. You may cross off each letter of the alphabet as you use it because each one will be used just once. As an example, the letter H has been added to the first word to make SCHOOL.

A B C D E F G H I J K L M N O P Q R S T U V W X Y Z

1. S C H O O L
2. F A V O R S
3. T O __ A T O
4. L I __ U I D
5. C A __ A R Y
6. W I __ K E D
7. Y O __ U R T
8. H I __ A C K
9. I N __ O R M
10. C A __ T O N
11. S T __ D E N T
12. M E __ I C O
13. F L __ I N G

14. H A __ I T S
15. G R __ D E D
16. R E __ C U E
17. D O __ E N S
18. P R __ F I T
19. V O __ E L S
20. T R __ P L E
21. B A __ E R Y
22. S T __ A D Y
23. E X __ E C T
24. C A __ M E R
25. F U __ U R E
26. J U __ G E S

# Trivia Quiz

Each question comes with four possible answers.
Circle the correct one.

1. Which of these animals has the most legs?

   chipmunk       stork       (spider)       honeybee

2. The Pentagon building is just outside of which U.S. city?

   Washington, D.C.       New York City       Los Angeles       Boston

3. Which of these things was invented first?

   cell phone       cable TV       DVD player       (radio)

4. Which of these athletes does *not* wear a face mask?

   hockey goalie       baseball catcher       fencer       tennis player

5. What shape is also the name of a musical instrument?

   square       (triangle)       circle       rectangle

6. What do you call the center of a hurricane?

   arm       (eye)       nose       throat

Answers on page 275

# Missing Link

The zookeeper's binoculars were stolen while he was cleaning the monkey cage. Follow the path to the mischievous monkey to get them back.

Answer on page 275

# Trees Crisscross

Every word in this list is the name of a tree.
Place each word into the grid. Start with the letters that
are already in the grid. One word will lead to another until
the whole grid is filled.

**3 Letters**
Ash
Elm
Gum

**4 Letters**
Lime
Plum

**5 Letters**
Apple
Guava
Maple
Olive

**6 Letters**
Laurel
Litchi
Mimosa
Orange
Papaya
Spruce
Walnut

**7 Letters**
Juniper
Redwood

**8 Letters**
Sycamore

Grid letters: G, O, P, L, E

Answers on page 275

120

# The IN Crowd

Each of the words in this puzzle begins with the letters IN. Can you get INto it? Put one letter after the first IN, two letters after the second IN, right up to ten letters after the last IN. The clues in parentheses will help.

1. IN __ (Pen filler)

2. IN __ __ (One-twelfth of a foot)

3. IN __ __ __ (The finger next to your thumb)

4. IN __ __ __ __ (Harm from an accident)

5. IN __ __ __ __ __ (Opposite of outside)

6. IN __ __ __ __ __ __ (Where to go to get e-mail)

7. IN __ __ __ __ __ __ __ (Unable to be seen)

8. IN __ __ __ __ __ __ __ __ (Like a failed pass in football)

9. IN __ __ __ __ __ __ __ __ __ (Data)

10. IN __ __ __ __ __ __ __ __ __ __ (The U.S. Declaration of this)

Answers on page 275

# Country Balloons

In each balloon is the name of a country minus one letter. Find the missing letters that complete each name, and write it on the blank line. Then arrange those missing letters to spell another country.

1. _____ 6. _____

2. _____ 7. _____

3. _____ 8. _____

4. _____ 9. _____

5. _____

1.

2.

3.

4.

5.

6.

7.

8.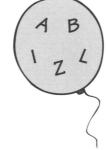

9.

Answer: _____

Answers on page 275

# Find the Missing Letters

Fill in the two missing middle letters in each of the following words. The clues will help you figure them out. Hint: The second letter of each word is a vowel—*a, e, i, o,* or *u.*

1. B __ __ t (You row it.)
   B __ __ t (It holds up your pants.)
   B __ __ t (Homer Simpson's son.)

2. C __ __ t (A horse draws it.)
   C __ __ t (You wear it.)
   C __ __ t (A baby horse.)

3. D __ __ t (You throw it at a bull's-eye.)
   D __ __ t (It's in a car after an accident.)
   D __ __ t (You wash it off if you get it on you.)

4. F __ __ t (You run at this speed.)
   F __ __ t (You punch with it.)
   F __ __ t (You use logs to build it for protection.)

5. M __ __ t (You have to.)
   M __ __ t (You shake hands when you do this.)
   M __ __ t (You see this water around a castle.)

Answers on page 276

# One Word, Different Meanings

Write the one word that fits all the blanks
in each set of sentences.

1. My father works at a factory that makes tubes and
_____ for bicycles. He has been there for many years, but
he never _____ of his work.

2. Jan gasped when she saw a large _____ in her yard.
She could hardly _____ the thought of the animal
ruining her flowers.

3. Mrs. Blake _____ do many things. During the summer,
she likes to _____ peaches. A store-bought _____
of peaches just _____ not compare with Mrs. Blake's.

4. The present was _____ and easy to carry. Dana turned
on the _____ so she could see better. When she opened her
gift, she found a _____ blue scarf and a silver necklace.

5. Kevin used a piece of chalk to draw a straight _____ on
the sidewalk. Then he told his friends to _____ up behind
him. The _____ of children then hopped on one foot along
the chalk mark.

6. Each boy carried a _____ on his back during the hike.
When the boys got back to their tents, Trent took out a
_____ of gum. "My mom told me to _____ gum in
my bag and share it," he said.

Answers on page 276

# What Am I?

Here's a countdown of 10 statements about one thing. How many will it take you to figure out what it is?

10. People laugh when I'm *good*.

9. You can play one of me, but I'm not a game or sport or musical instrument.

8. Sometimes I'm really silly.

7. People usually don't take me seriously.

6. I can be an ice breaker.

5. You can tell me.

4. Some people get rich and famous for telling me.

3. I don't always start out funny, but I'm best when I end that way.

2. Sometimes I start with "Knock knock."

1. I'm four letters long, and I start with a *J*.

Answer on page 276

# A Learning Experience

Place the various school-related words in the list into the grid so they interlock as in a crossword. When you are done, all the words will have been used exactly once. (Ignore any spaces between the words; for example, enter SPELLING BEE as SPELLINGBEE.)

**3 Letters**
Art
Pen

**4 Letters**
Desk
Test

**5 Letters**
Class
Essay
Exams
Globe
Lunch
Music
Pupil
Tardy
Write

**6 Letters**
Eraser

**7 Letters**
Courses
English

Library
Pencils
Scholar
Student

**9 Letters**
Cafeteria

**11 Letters**
Spelling bee

Answers on page 276

# Mix and Match Again

Rearrange the letters in each word on the left so you can add it to the word on the right to form a new word. (This first set is easy, but be prepared! It will get harder as you move along.)

1. CARE _____TRACK
2. GRIN _____LEADER
3. STAKE _____BOARD
4. POST _____WATCH
5. SEAT _____BOUND

Now try a matching game!
Rearrange the letters in the numbered list to form a new word with *any* of the words on the right.

1. FILE _____BOAT
2. BRAKE _____LET
3. CARS _____TIME
4. MATES _____KNOB
5. ODOR _____FAST

Now try it in reverse!

1. _____CAST      CAPES
2. _____SOME     PART
3. _____DOOR     MILE
4. _____LIGHT    BOARD
5. _____SHIP     THERE

Answers on page 276

# Add-ons

Add a word to each word below to make a new word with a different meaning. Use the clues to help you.

1. Add the opposite of high to make a word that means under. be_____

2. Add a body part to make a word that means good looking. _____some.

3. Add vegetable kernels to make a snack at the movie theater. pop_____

4. Add a word that means to steal to make a songbird. _____in

5. Add a jar's cover to make something hard. so_____

6. Add an auto to make a small cardboard box. _____ton

7. Add 24 hours to make the day after yesterday. to_____

8. Add a cut tree trunk to make a way crowded. _____jam

9. Add what's in a sentence to make something that will get your computer to work. pass_____

10. Add a group of wolves to make a parcel sent by the post office. _____age

11. Add a plane's wheel to make what you wear. at_____

12. Add something that unlocks a door to make an animal you can ride. don_____

13. Add a big pig to make nonsense. _____wash

14. Add how old you are to make a strip to cover a cut. band_____

Answers on page 276

# At the Plate

Find the words and phrases listed on the left in the word search grid (which is shaped like home plate!) Words can be across, backward, up, down, or diagonal, but they are always in a straight line. Circle the words as you find them, and cross them off the list. When you're done, read the uncircled letters in the grid from left to right, top to bottom, to spell out three more baseball terms.

**Word list**

At bat
Bunt
Double play
Dugout
Error
Fair
Foul
Hits
Home run
Infield
Innings
Pitcher's mound
Runs
Safe
Stolen base
Strike
Umpire
Walk
World Series
You're out

```
D L E I F N I S K Y P I T
E O E S A B N E L O T S U
F O U L N H C I A U H G O
A H I B T O T R W R E N G
S H A R L M B E A E U I U
P I T C H E R S M O U N D
L T B L S R P D H U O N S
  S A U O U U L F T R I
    T R N N M R A T S
      R T T P O I Y
        I O I W R
          K R P
            E
```

Answers: _____

Answers on page 276

# Number Challenge

Fill in this crossword with numbers instead of letters. Start with 1-Across, a simple multiplication problem (which you can probably do in your head). Using a calculator or just your brain, figure out the answers to the rest of the Across clues. Then check your math using the Down clues.

## Across

1. 9 x 2
3. 1-Across plus 101
6. 1-Across times 4
7. 6-Across times 100
8. 7-Across plus 312
10. 1-Across plus 6-Across
11. 3-Across plus 214
13. One-half of 10-Across
15. 7-Across plus 135
18. 15-Across minus 5
20. 1 more than 1-Across
21. 11-Across plus 7
22. 1-Across plus 13-Across

## Down

1. 11-Across minus 156
2. 21-Across plus 485
3. 1-Across minus 6
4. 22-Across plus 46
5. 13-Across times 20
7. 15-Across times 9 plus 6,355
9. 3-Down plus 1
12. 20-Across plus 14
13. 2-Down minus 352
14. 13-Down plus 61
16. 14-Down minus 218
17. 16-Down plus 277
19. 10-Across minus 60

Answers on page 276

# Surroundings

Put one of the four-letter words from the box into the blank spaces around each letter grouping to make a longer word. Use the clues in parentheses.
We did the first one for you.

COAT    COST    DARE    MANE    MILE
NEST    PAGE    PARE    POST    PUSH
REAL    SHOO    SHOW    TALE

1. _C O_ P Y C _A T_    (unoriginal person)
2. __ __ N T E __ __    (a competition)
3. __ __ C K A __ __    (container)
4. __ __ O R E __ __    (having the least money)
5. __ __ D P O __ __    (young frog)
6. __ __ A L L __ __    (not deep)
7. __ __ R A C __ __    (an amazing event)
8. __ __ C I T __ __    (public performance)
9. __ __ C H I __ __    (mechanical device)
10. __ __ B L I __ __    (produce a book or newspaper)
11. __ __ A M P __ __    (soap for the hair)
12. __ __ S T U __ __    (field where cows graze)
13. __ __ A R E __ __    (closest)
14. __ __ Y C A __ __    (center for young children)

Answers on page 276

# A Word Train

Read the clues, and write the matching words. Use the last two letters of the previous word to begin the next word.

1. an animal with stripes    _Zebra_
2. comes after a storm    _rainbow_
3. had an obligation to pay    _owed_
4. end of a cliff    _wedge_
5. leader of an army    _general_
6. nearly    _almost_
7. a place to get gas    _station_
8. one time    _once_
9. middle    _center_
10. remove a pencil mark    _erase_
11. it goes up and down    _see saw_
12. fantastic    _awesome_
13. not nice    _mean_
14. it keeps a ship from drifting    _anchor_
15. command    _order_

Answers on page 276

# Flowers Galore!

Place each flower name in the appropriate set of boxes. Continue until all the boxes are filled. We put chrysanthemum in place to get you started.

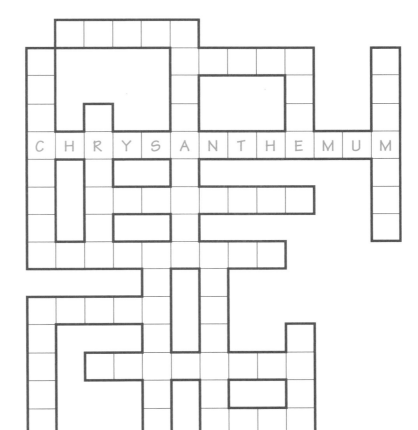

C H R Y S A N T H E M U M

**4 Letters**
Iris
Rose

**5 Letters**
Aster
Daisy
Lilac
Poppy
Phlox

**6 Letters**
Orchid

**7 Letters**
Alyssum
Anemone

**8 Letters**
Gardenia
Hibiscus
Hyacinth
Wisteria

**9 Letters**
Carnation
Hydrangea

**13 Letters**
~~Chrysanthemum~~

Answers on page 276

# Tourist Attractions

Oops! A new worker at the USA visitors center removed three-letter words from 12 major tourist attractions. Each missing word was rounded up and put into the box below. Can you put each word into an empty space to name the real attractions?

| | | | |
|---|---|---|---|
| ACE | BET | CAT | COT |
| ELL | HIT | IRE | LIB |
| OLD | RAN | TOW | USE |

1. __ __ __ S Y   R O S S   H O U S E (Philadelphia)

2. A L __ __ __ R A Z   I S L A N D (San Francisco)

3. E M P __ __ __   S T A T E   B U I L D I N G (New York City)

4. E P __ __ __   C E N T E R (Orlando)

5. F __ __ __ K L I N   I N S T I T U T E (Philadelphia)

6. G E T T Y   M __ __ __ U M (Los Angeles)

7. G __ __ __ E N   G A T E   B R I D G E (San Francisco)

8. L I B E R T Y   B __ __ __ (Philadelphia)

9. S E A R S   __ __ __ E R (Chicago)

10. S P __ __ __   N E E D L E (Seattle)

11. S T A T U E   O F   __ __ __ E R T Y (New York City)

12. W __ __ __ E   H O U S E (Washington, D.C.)

Answers on page 276

# Crossword

## Across

1. _ _ _ Vegas, Nevada
4. Money left for the server
7. _ _ _ bad mood: 2 words
8. Perform
11. What the bride and groom say at a wedding: 2 words
12. Pepper _ _ _ (TV cartoon)
13. One of the signs of the zodiac
14. _ _ _ can
15. Decay
16. "_ _ _ good turn deserves another."
17. A piece of wood in the fireplace
18. Rich person's boat
20. Teacher's _ _ _
21. Lift up
23. Tampa _ _ _ (inlet in Florida)
25. Jewel found inside an oyster
28. It holds a hamburger
29. Insect that makes honey
30. Long, skinny fish
32. Part of an omelet
33. Not even
34. "How _ _ _ supposed to know?": 2 words
35. Ginger _ _ _ (fizzy drink)
36. What a nod means
37. Pro and _ _ _ (sides in a debate)
38. Dover is its capital: Abbreviation
39. Explosive stuff: Abbreviation

## Down

1. Fibber
2. Bother
3. He lives at the North Pole
4. The name of a book
5. Really stupid person
6. Ping-_ _ _ _ (game)
8. Word that means "hello" and "good-bye" in Hawaii
9. Insect with many legs
10. Tic-tac-_ _ _
19. Weep
20. Small green vegetable
22. They're planted in a garden
23. Brass musical instrument
24. One who wears a halo
26. Respond to something
27. Sour yellow fruit
28. Small round thing on a necklace, sometimes
29. Young man
31. Pocket fuzz

Answers on page 277

135

# More Scrambled Sports

Use the clues to help you figure out the first two words in each puzzle. Then rearrange the letters of your answers to spell the name of a sport.

1. the thick, hairy coat of an animal     _ _ _ _

   to make music with your voice     _ _ _ _ _

   a sport in which people move across the
   water by standing on a board     _ _ _ _ _ _ _ _ _

2. a round object used in a game     _ _ _ _ _

   beautiful     _ _ _ _ _ _

   a sport in which players use
   their hands to hit a ball     _ _ _ _ _ _ _ _ _ _ _

3. Noah's boat     _ _ _ _

   a drink made from dried leaves     _ _ _

   a sport that is a form of self-defense     _ _ _ _ _ _ _

4. a steady, low light     _ _ _ _ _

   a large container     _ _ _

   a sport in which players use a heavy
   ball to knock down pins     _ _ _ _ _ _ _ _

5. a large, cheerful smile     _ _ _ _ _

   a woman who lives in a convent     _ _ _

   a sport in which people race on foot     _ _ _ _ _ _ _ _

Answers on page 277

# Word Magic

Change *saw* to *pen*. Change only one letter at a time. Use the picture clues to help you.

| S | A | W |
|---|---|---|
|   |   |   |
|   |   |   |
| P | E | N |

Now change *pin* to *toe*.

Now change *cap* to *tub*.

| P | I | N |
|---|---|---|
|   |   |   |
|   |   |   |
| T | O | E |

| C | A | P |
|---|---|---|
|   |   |   |
|   |   |   |
| T | U | B |

Answers on page 277

# Mystery Letters

Each sentence contains a group of capital letters. The letters stand for a familiar set of nouns. See if you can figure out what each set stands for.

1. Without ROYGBIV, rainbows wouldn't be so pretty.

   _____

2. WSSF helps break up the year.

   _____

3. Look into space for MVEMJSUNP.

   _____

4. MTWTFSS are weekly events.

   _____

5. Just look at your hand to help you count OTTFF.

   _____

6. If you want to sail the seas, you'll need to go on PAAI.

   _____

7. It's "great" to see these watery HOMES.

   _____

Answers on page 277

# Desert Crossing

Put each word into the grid in alphabetical order.
Then read down the starred column to find the four-word
answer to this joke: What should you carry with you on
a long hike through the desert?

Youthful
Catalog
Unit
Gerbil
Friend
Dough
Nearly
Kettle
Issue
Tickle
Radio
Branch
Opinion

# Word Maze

Go from *BEGIN* to *END* by drawing a path through the maze of words. You move by drawing a line from the word you're on to a word directly above, below, to the right, or to the left. Its first or last letter must either begin or end the next word. For example, to start, connect the word *BEGIN* to an adjoining word that starts or ends with *B* or *N*. The answer is *TURN*. Now connect *TURN* to a word that starts or ends with *T* or *N*. Continue that way until you reach *END*. You'll go through all 25 words just once.

| BEGIN | LEAD | DIM | DARTS | SNAKE |
|-------|------|-----|-------|-------|
| TURN | ROLL | JOKER | GRAB | SPRING |
| TUNA | ASK | JEEP | BINGO | OFF |
| YANKEE | KITTY | HELP | ZOOM | FUZZ |
| EARRING | ELBOW | WISH | MIND | END |

Answer on page 277

# Grand Opening

Each of the examples below is missing its first letter. Fill in the blanks with a letter of the alphabet to make a word. As you use each letter, cross it out in the alphabet below. Each letter will be used exactly once.

A B C D E F G H I J K L M N O P Q R S T U V W X Y Z

1. _____ URP
2. _____ ISTEN
3. _____ ELEPHONE
4. _____ OLIDAY
5. _____ UIZ
6. _____ RANDFATHER
7. _____ EOPLE
8. _____ OLLEYBALL
9. _____ RAGON
10. _____ ILVER
11. _____ RDER
12. _____ HICH
13. _____ PPLE

14. _____ UICE
15. _____ EIGHBOR
16. _____ LAGPOLE
17. _____ ASY
18. _____ EBRA
19. _____ YLOPHONE
20. _____ CICLE
21. _____ EINDEER
22. _____ SUALLY
23. _____ ISTLETOE
24. _____ OGURT
25. _____ RAZY
26. _____ ANGAROO

Answers on page 277

# City's Silly Phrases

The letters in the name of each six-letter U.S. city in the left column were rearranged into a nonsense phrase and placed randomly in the right column. Can you match each city with its silly anagram? Write the answer letter of the correct phrase in the blank space next to each city name.

| | | |
|---|---|---|
| 1. Albany | _____ | a. lie mob |
| 2. Boston | _____ | b. tee rex |
| 3. Dallas | _____ | c. we rank |
| 4. Dayton | _____ | d. sad one |
| 5. El Paso | _____ | e. real do |
| 6. Elmira | _____ | f. no cuts |
| 7. Exeter | _____ | g. and toy |
| 8. Laredo | _____ | h. all sad |
| 9. Mobile | _____ | i. me rail |
| 10. Newark | _____ | j. sob not |
| 11. Sedona | _____ | k. so pale |
| 12. Tucson | _____ | l. any lab |

Answers on page 277

# Mixed Messages

Here are three riddles:

1. What is taken before you get it?

2. What do you call a dog without a tail?

3. Where do math teachers go to eat?

The answers to these riddles are hidden in the box below.
To find them, copy all the letters above the numeral 1.
Go in order from left to right and top to bottom,
and put each letter into a blank space below.
Do the same thing for the numerals 2 and 3.

| Y | A | T | O | T | O | H |
|---|---|---|---|---|---|---|
| 1 | 2 | 3 | 3 | 3 | 1 | 2 |
| O | H | U | E | R | L | T |
| 2 | 3 | 1 | 3 | 1 | 3 | 2 |
| U | P | N | I | C | C | H |
| 3 | 1 | 3 | 1 | 3 | 1 | 3 |
| D | O | T | C | U | O | U |
| 2 | 2 | 1 | 3 | 1 | 3 | 3 |
| N | R | T | G | E | E | R |
| 3 | 1 | 3 | 2 | 3 | 1 | 3 |

Answer to Riddle 1: __ __ __ __   __ __ __ __ __ __ __

Answer to Riddle 2: __   __ __ __   __ __ __

Answer to Riddle 3: __ __   __ __ __   __ __ __ __ __

__ __ __ __ __ __ __ __

Answers on page 277

# Silly Rhymes

Your job is to name a well-known person, place, group, movie, event, or fictional character that rhymes with the silly phrase in the left column. You have the first letters of each answer word and the number of letters in each word. Check out the clues at the bottom of the page, which are in no particular order.

1. Bella Dare      D <u>E</u> <u>L</u> <u>A</u> <u>W</u> <u>A</u> <u>R</u> <u>E</u>

2. *Lease Zither Moon*      R _ _ _ _    W _ _ _ _ _ _ _ _ _ _

3. Gabe Tooth      B _ _ _    R _ _ _ _

4. *Geeky Dry Way*      F _ _ _ _ _ _    F _ _ _ _ _ _

5. Neater Man      P _ _ _ _    P _ _

6. *Mack Greet Toys*      B _ _ _ _ _ _ _ _ _ _    B _ _ _ _

7. How Cow      B _ _    W _ _

8. *Due Pork Thicks*      N _ _   Y _ _ _ _   K _ _ _ _ _

9. Dance Farm Wrong      L _ _ _ _ _    A _ _ _ _ _ _ _ _

10. *Hill Mates*      B _ _ _ _    G _ _ _ _ _

11. Faint Tall      S _ _ _ _ _    P _ _ _ _

12. *Trooper Goal*      S _ _ _ _ _    B _ _ _ _

CLUES

Actress who starred in *Legally Blonde* and *Just Like Heaven*
Basketball team
Boy band with the hit song "Incomplete"
Very rich founder of Microsoft
Capital of Minnesota
Cyclist who won the Tour de France seven times
Fictional boy who refuses to grow up
Major football event
Movie about a mother and daughter switching places
One of the greatest baseball players of all time
Rapper whose name sounds like a dog's bark
Small state

Answers on page 277

# Start/Finish

Figure out the four-letter word that answers each clue, and put it into the grid at the matching number. Some words will start at the starred line, and other words will end at the starred line. When you have entered all the words, read across to find the answer to this joke: What kind of lotion do monsters wear at the beach?

CLUES

1. In a restaurant you order food from a __ __ __ __
2. Baby goats are called __ __ __ __
3. A person who doesn't tell the truth is a __ __ __ __
4. The largest continent is __ __ __ __
5. You go to a mall to __ __ __ __ for items
6. __ __ __ __ blue is a very dark color
7. Use the phone to make a __ __ __ __
8. If you are "green with __ __ __ __ ," it means you are jealous
9. A postal worker delivers the __ __ __ __ to your house

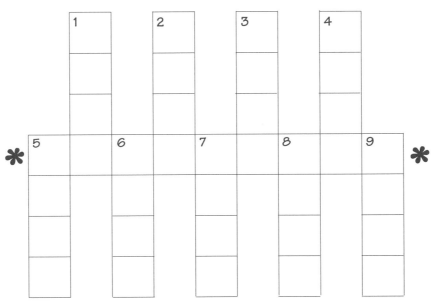

Answers on page 278

# Word Pyramids

Begin by writing a letter in the top box. Fill in the remaining boxes in the following rows. Each row contains all the letters in the row above it plus one more letter. The letters will always remain in the same order.

1. best grade
2. placed before a vowel sound
3. moved quickly on foot
4. falls from clouds
5. runs on rails
6. exert great effort

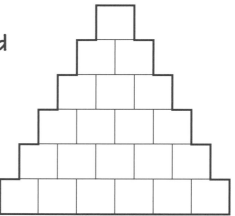

1. me
2. a thing
3. hole in the ground
4. saliva
5. malice
6. an elf or a fairy

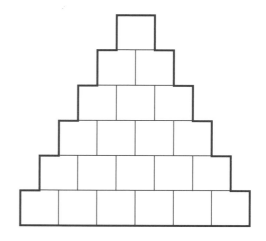

Answers on page 278

# Fivers

Five 5-letter birds are hidden in the mini grid below. To find them, use one letter from each column going from left to right. Each letter will be used only once, so circle it after you use it. The first one has been done for you.

Birds
1. RAVEN
2. _____
3. _____
4. _____
5. _____

| R | A | B | E | K |
|---|---|---|---|---|
| G | O | V | I | E |
| R | T | O | L | N |
| S | A | O | R | E |
| E | O | G | S | N |

In the next grid there are five 5-letter foreign countries to be found. Again, use one letter from each column going from left to right.

Foreign countries
1. _____
2. _____
3. _____
4. _____
5. _____

| I | G | P | I | N |
|---|---|---|---|---|
| J | H | A | A | A |
| E | P | D | P | A |
| C | A | I | I | T |
| S | N | Y | N | N |

Answers on page 278

# Magic Word Squares

Magic word squares read the same both across and down. Answer each clue with a five-letter word, and write it in the grid twice—once going across and once going down.

Across and Down
1. Lightning flashes
2. City in Nebraska
3. Tag on clothing
4. Not those
5. Bargain events in stores

Across and Down
1. Walked in shallow water
2. Not below
3. There are 12 eggs in one
4. Happening
5. Marks in a car fender

Across and Down
1. Person on the runway at a fashion show
2. Musical play
3. Cause to be late
4. Use one end of a pencil
5. A birthday cake often has a top and bottom _ _ _ _ _ with filling in between

Answers on page 278

# What's Going On?

Look carefully at the examples. Each line of numbers is a separate example. See if you can figure out how to get from one number to the next. Once you've figured it out, complete the remaining sets of numbers in the same way.

Examples:

12 ⟶ 3
45 ⟶ 9
231 ⟶ 7
96 ⟶ 15 ⟶ 6
764 ⟶ 17 ⟶ 8

1. 43 ⟶ _____

2. 18 ⟶ _____

3. 60 ⟶ _____

4. 78 ⟶ _____ ⟶ _____

5. 94 ⟶ _____ ⟶ _____

6. 416 ⟶ _____ ⟶ _____

7. 2,577 ⟶ _____ ⟶ _____

8. 1,468 ⟶ _____ ⟶ _____ ⟶ _____

9. 3,899 ⟶ _____ ⟶ _____ ⟶ _____

10. 4,987 ⟶ _____ ⟶ _____ ⟶ _____

Answers on page 278

# Put in a Good Word for Me

The clues in parentheses tell you what three-letter words to put in the blanks. These short words will create longer words when added to the existing letters. In this puzzle, all the combined words are titles of people.

1. ___ ___ ___ O R          (month after April)
2. ___ ___ ___ RIFF          (not he)
3. ___ ___ ___ E          (title for a lord)
4. ___ ___ ___ L          (what you use to hear with)
5. ___ ___ ___ DINAL          (one unit of a train)
6. ___ ___ ___ TAIN          (baseball player's hat)
7. ___ ___ ___ E          (slang for dad)
8. ___ ___ ___ UTENANT          (not tell the truth)

Answers on page 278

# Add Another Word

Each of the following four words can have the same three-letter word added to them to make new words. Find that three-letter word.

\_\_ \_\_ \_\_ side

\_\_ \_\_ \_\_ ice

\_\_ \_\_ \_\_ beat

\_\_ \_\_ \_\_ end

Find another three-letter word to add to these four words.

\_\_ \_\_ \_\_ don

\_\_ \_\_ \_\_ rot

\_\_ \_\_ \_\_ king

\_\_ \_\_ \_\_ able

Now here's a hard one to find.

\_\_ \_\_ \_\_ way

\_\_ \_\_ \_\_ due

\_\_ \_\_ \_\_ lime

\_\_ \_\_ \_\_ side

Answers on page 278

# Crossword

## Across

1. Not good
4. Old cloth used for dusting
7. Go _ _ _ vacation: 2 words
8. Word ending that means "sort of"
9. It holds back water in a river
12. Strange
13. Enjoy a winter sport
14. Cheer for a bullfighter
15. City in Florida
17. Tokyo's country
19. Number that appears on a penny
21. Geeky person
22. Monkey bars: 2 words
25. Not straight
26. Distant
27. "Honesty _ _ _ _ _ best policy": 2 words
29. It's poured over waffles
33. "Just _ _ _ thought!": 2 words
34. Struck a match
36. Had a snack
37. "_ _ _ you later, alligator!"
38. He runs a bar on *The Simpsons*
39. Sound made by a woodpecker
40. Your and my
41. That lady

## Down

1. Sound of an explosion
2. Me, myself, _ _ _ _: 2 words
3. How a baby might say "father"
4. Moving up
5. Have a question
6. Letters after F
9. One of the Seven Dwarfs
10. _ _ _ _ _ clock (item that can wake you up)
11. Heal
16. 1/12 of a year
18. Really upset

20. One of Santa's assistants

22. _ _ _ _ _ James (famous outlaw)

23. Remove a knot

24. Holiday with bunnies and eggs

25. Prejudice

28. Red Muppet

30. "Darn it!"

31. State with the Great Salt Lake

32. _ _ _ _ Le Pew (cartoon skunk)

35. Paper that shows a debt

|   1 | 2 | 3 |   | 4 | 5 | 6 |   |   |    |    |
|-----|---|---|---|---|---|---|---|---|----|----|
| 7   |   |   |   | 8 |   |   |   | 9 | 10 | 11 |
| 12  |   |   |   | 13|   |   |   |14 |    |    |
| 15  |   |   |16 |   |   |17 |18 |   |    |    |
|     |   |   |19 |   |20 |   |21 |   |    |    |
|     |22 |23 |   |   |   |24 |   |   |    |    |
| 25  |   |   |   |   |26 |   |   |   |    |    |
| 27  |   |   |   |28 |   |29 |   |30 |31  |32  |
| 33  |   |   |   |34 |35 |   |   |36 |    |    |
| 37  |   |   |   |38 |   |   |   |39 |    |    |
|     |   |   |   |40 |   |   |   |41 |    |    |

Answers on page 278

# Clued In

Answer each clue, and write the word in the numbered spaces. Then put each letter into the spaces in the Riddle box, making sure that you match the numbers. Work back and forth between the clues and the Riddle box to find something to laugh at!

Clues

The opposite of sit

$\overline{18}\ \overline{22}\ \overline{29}\ \overline{7}\ \overline{17}$

Had a meal

$\overline{3}\ \overline{10}\ \overline{40}$

Large

$\overline{37}\ \overline{25}\ \overline{28}$

The color of most marshmallows

$\overline{14}\ \overline{2}\ \overline{38}\ \overline{19}\ \overline{12}$

Slice of browned bread

$\overline{11}\ \overline{15}\ \overline{31}\ \overline{23}\ \overline{26}$

Paintings and sculpture

$\overline{20}\ \overline{16}\ \overline{33}$

Do this with an oar

$\overline{13}\ \overline{34}\ \overline{1}$

Not sick

$\overline{24}\ \overline{9}\ \overline{8}\ \overline{39}$

Where your lips and teeth are

$\overline{35}\ \overline{36}\ \overline{32}\ \overline{5}\ \overline{27}$

Take a break to relax

$\overline{21}\ \overline{6}\ \overline{30}\ \overline{4}$

---

Riddle box

$\overline{1}\ \overline{2}\ \overline{3}\ \overline{4}\quad \overline{5}\ \overline{6}\ \overline{7}\ ^-\ \overline{8}\ \overline{9}\ \overline{10}\ \overline{11}\ \overline{12}\ \overline{13}$

$\overline{14}\ \overline{15}\ \overline{16}\ \overline{17}\quad \overline{18}\ \overline{19}\ \overline{20}\ \overline{21}\ \overline{22}\ \overline{23}\quad \overline{24}\ \overline{25}\ \overline{26}\ \overline{27}$

$\overline{28}\ \overline{29}\ \overline{30}\ ^?\quad \overline{31}\ \overline{32}\ \overline{33}\ \overline{34}\ \overline{35}\ \overline{36}\ \overline{37}\ \overline{38}\ \overline{39}\ \overline{40}\ .$

Answers on page 278

# Hotel Pool Scene

The drawing on this page is really three puzzles in one!
Test your powers of observation by completing
the following activities.

1. Circle 5 things that begin with the letter S.

2. Find 5 things that are wrong with this picture.

3. There are 6 letters hidden around the pool area. Find
   them, and then unscramble them to form a sound that
   is heard around the pool all day.

Answers on page 278

# Trivia Quiz

Each question comes with four possible answers.
Circle the correct answer.

1. In which of these games do you use tiles with letters on them?

Scrabble          Monopoly          Poker          Chess

2. In a rainbow, what color comes between blue and violet?

Red          Indigo          Green          Silver

3. Which of these equations has an answer greater than the other equations?

8 x 9          46 + 27          112 - 41          280 ÷ 4

4. The world's highest mountain is Mount Everest. On which continent is Mount Everest found?

Asia          Africa          South America          Europe

5. Freckles are least likely to be found on which of these body parts?

Forearms          Back          Soles of the feet          Face

6. Which of these sports events is held once every four years?

Super Bowl          Indy 500          World Series          Winter Olympics

Answers on page 278

# Tarzanna's Treehouse

Help Tarzanna get back to her home in the tree.

Answer on page 279

# Confused Compounds

There's something wrong with each of the compound words below. Replace the underlined words with their opposites to correct the compound words.

1. manbug _____

2. downset _____

3. longcut _____

4. weekbegin _____

5. infit _____

6. overground _____

7. handsit _____

8. frontfire _____

9. daygown _____

10. flashdark _____

11. looserope _____

12. blackbottom _____

13. fastpoke _____

14. faresick _____

15. nearaway _____

16. golight _____

Answers on page 279

# Music Makers

Write the names of the musical instruments in the boxes.
(Hint: Start with the instrument that has seven letters.)

**4 Letters**
Drum
Harp
Tuba

**5 Letters**
Banjo
Cello
Flute
Organ
Piano

**6 Letters**
Cymbal
Guitar
Violin

**7 Letters**
Trumpet

**8 Letters**
Clarinet
Trombone

**9 Letters**
Saxophone
Xylophone

Answers on page 279

# Famous Americans

Use the letters above the diagrams to fill in the empty squares. The word across is the first name of a famous American, and the word down is that person's last name. The letter in the center square is part of both names.

1.   EEEIPRSSVY

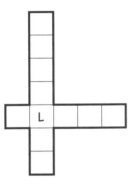

3.   AHKNNOR

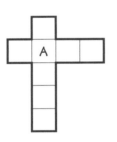

2.   AEILMMNNOOY

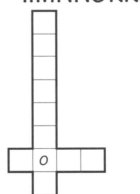

4.   IIMNNORRST

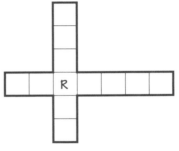

5.   AEEGHINNOORSTW

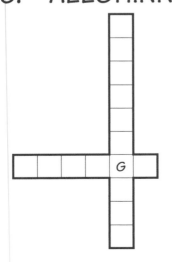

6.   AEELLNOOORRSTV

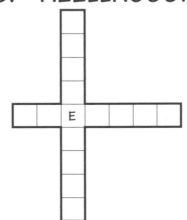

Answers on page 279

# Categories

This puzzle is based on the old game Categories. In each box, write the name of something that belongs to the category on the left and also starts with the letter at the top. We've filled in one example to get you going.

| | A | B | C | G | S |
|---|---|---|---|---|---|
| Fruits | APPLE | | | | |
| Musical Instruments | | | | | |
| Family Relatives | | | | | |
| 4-Letter Words Ending in Y | | | | | |

Answers on page 279

# Clued In

Answer each clue, and write the word in the numbered spaces. Then put each letter into the spaces in the joke box, making sure that you match up the numbers. Work back and forth between the clues and the joke box to find something to laugh at!

Clues

The opposite of left

$\underline{\phantom{5}}\phantom{x}\underline{\phantom{24}}\phantom{x}\underline{\phantom{10}}\phantom{x}\underline{\phantom{2}}\phantom{x}\underline{\phantom{26}}$
5   24   10   2   26

The opposite of hard

$\underline{\phantom{9}}\phantom{x}\underline{\phantom{3}}\phantom{x}\underline{\phantom{32}}\phantom{x}\underline{\phantom{13}}$
9   3   32   13

Uses a chair

14   11   17   25

Come in first in a race

1   6   29

Outdoor game played with clubs

8   16   33   12

Exam

15   19   36   30

Wooden stick used in baseball

4   31   23

Face part used for smelling

7   34   27   21

Body parts with fingers

18   28   22   20   35

Joke box

___ ___ ___   ___ ___ ___ ___ ___ ___   ___ ___ ___ ___ ___
1   2   3     4   5   6   7   8   9      10  11  12  13  14
                                                    ?

___ ___   ___ ___ ___   ___ ___ ___ ___ ___ ___ ___
15  16    17  18  19    20  21  22  23  24  25  26

___ ___ ___ ___ ___   ___ ___ ___ ___ ___ .
27  28  29  30  31     32  33  34  35  36

Answers on page 279

# Paint a Picture

Find a hidden picture in this grid by coloring in the correct squares in each row. For example, in Row 1, color in square C. When you're done, you'll find something you might take on a trip.

Row 1    C
Row 2    C, D, E, F, J, K, L
Row 3    E, K
Row 4    E, F, G, H, I, J, K
Row 5    E, K

Row 6    D, F, J, L
Row 7    B, C, G, J, M, N
Row 8    A, B, C, D, H, I, J, K, L, M, N, O
Row 9    A, B, C, D, L, M, N, O
Row 10   B, C, M, N

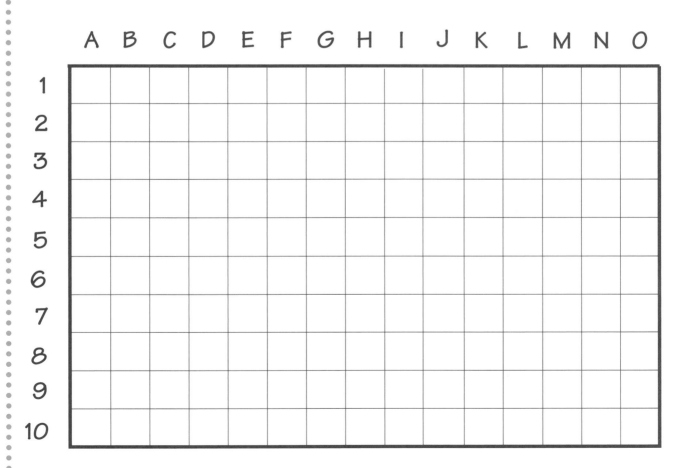

Answer on page 279

# Three-Letter Challenge

Fill in the boxes so that each vertical column contains a three-letter word. Use the letters in the clouds to help you. If you choose the letters in each set correctly, the ones in each center row will spell the name of a country.

1.

| O | T | G | A | I | W |
|---|---|---|---|---|---|
|   |   |   |   |   |   |
| F | Y | S | T | E | B |

C F E N A R N

2.

| F | O | E | A | W | E | A |
|---|---|---|---|---|---|---|
|   |   |   |   |   |   |   |
| R | E | L | L | S | D | D |

I A N L D R E

3.

| P | A | D | S | A |
|---|---|---|---|---|
|   |   |   |   |   |
| N | E | E | Y | E |

Y T G E P

4.

| A | C | U | A | P | C |
|---|---|---|---|---|---|
|   |   |   |   |   |   |
| E | P | E | K | G | N |

I A U S S R

5.

| S | T | J | R | F | M | O | A |
|---|---|---|---|---|---|---|---|
|   |   |   |   |   |   |   |   |
| Y | E | R | D | Y | T | E | D |

L T A D N H A I

Answers on page 279

# Troubles at Home

Can you find ten or more errors in this scene?

Answers on page 279

# True/False

Read each statement, and decide if it's true or false. If it's true, circle the letter in the True column; if it's false, circle the letter in the False column. When you've circled all the letters, read them from 1 to 13 to find the name of a popular children's author.

|  | True | False |
|---|---|---|
| 6 Pierre is the capital of Wyoming | I | (Y) |
| 13 Airplanes are kept in hangars | T | (L) |
| 11 The Camden family is featured on the TV show *7th Heaven* | K | C |
| 4 If you're in the "land of Nod," it means you're moving your head | (E) | O |
| 12 "Mona Lisa" was painted by Paul Gauguin | O | (E) |
| 7 A group of lions is called a pride | (S) | G |
| 1 Dr. Alexander Fleming discovered penicillin | L | S |
| 8 Fortune cookies are associated with Italian food | T | (N) |
| 2 The Earth is the third planet from the sun | (E) | O |
| 5 Lance Armstrong won 7 consecutive Tour de France bike races | N | C |
| 10 Leeks are related to onions | (C) | D |
| 9 Notre Dame cathedral is in Cologne, Germany | E | I |
| 3 Saturn is a planet in the solar system | (M) | B |

$\overline{\phantom{xx}}\ \overline{\phantom{xx}}\ \overline{\phantom{xx}}\ \overline{\phantom{xx}}\ \overline{\phantom{xx}}\ \overline{\phantom{xx}}\quad\overline{\phantom{xx}}\ \overline{\phantom{xx}}\ \overline{\phantom{xx}}\ \overline{\phantom{xx}}\ \overline{\phantom{xx}}\ \overline{\phantom{xx}}\ \overline{\phantom{xx}}$

1　2　3　4　5　6　　7　8　9　10　11　12　13

Answers on page 279

# School Daze

Oops. Someone took a three-letter word out of 12 school-related words and put the words into the box below. Can you get good marks by putting each word from the box into one of the empty spaces below to make a word related to the subjects, activities, and people found in schools? Cross off each word as you use it.

| | | | |
|---|---|---|---|
| AGE | ALL | CAR | CAT |
| EAR | HOW | MEN | OAR |
| PEN | SUB | TEN | TIN |

1. T E S __ __ __ G

2. P H Y S I C A L  E D U __ __ __ I O N

3. S __ __ __  A N D  T E L L

4. S T U D Y  H __ __ __ __

5. F O R E I G N  L A N G U __ __ __ __

6. C H A L K B __ __ __ __ D

7. R E P O R T  __ __ __ __ D

8. E L E __ __ __ __ T A R Y  S C H O O L

9. K I N D E R G A R __ __ __ __

10. __ __ __ __ S T I T U T E  T E A C H E R

11. __ __ __ __ M A N S H I P

12. R E S __ __ __ __ C H  P A P E R

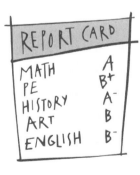

REPORT CARD

| MATH | A |
| PE | B+ |
| HISTORY | A- |
| ART | B |
| ENGLISH | B- |

Answers on page 280

# Start/Finish Rhymes

Figure out the four-letter word that rhymes with the given word by using the clue in parentheses. Example: In #1 the given word is *BLOB*, and the clue is (messy person). The answer word is *SLOB*. Write this word into the grid at the matching number. Some words will start at the starred line, and other words will end at the starred line. When you have entered all the words, read across to find the three-word answer to this riddle: What bird never uses a comb?

Clues

1. BLOB (messy person)
2. SAIL (bucket)
3. LIKE (2-wheeler)
4. SING (finger jewelry)
5. BITE (flying toy)
6. TAPES (monkeys)
7. PAGES (gets older)
8. FISH (plate)
9. PACES (high cards)
10. DAWN (grassy area)

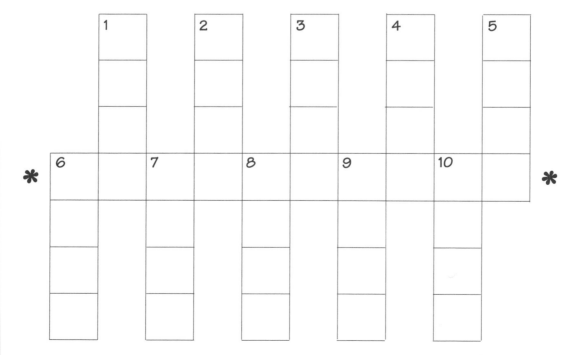

Answers on page 280

# Letters and Shapes

Form eight words by filling in the shapes with the given letters. You'll first have to figure out the letter that goes in each shape. We've given you one letter to help you.

### 1. n   a   r   i   g

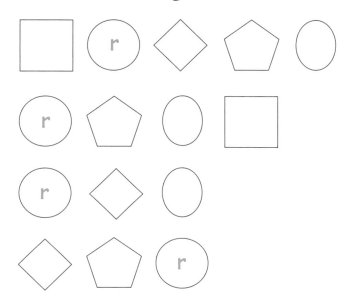

### 2. l   a   c   r   e

Answers on page 280

# A Word Train

Read the clues, and write the corresponding words on the blanks. Use the last two letters of the previous word to begin the next word. We did the first one for you.

1. continent ................................ _Africa_

2. coffee shop .............................. café

3. three in a yard .......................... feet

4. racial or cultural group ................. ethnic

5. frozen water drip ........................ icicle

6. it's in an envelope ...................... letter

7. baseball mistake ......................... error

8. carrot color ............................. orange

9. authentic ............................... genuine

10. birds' home ............................ nest

11. serious ................................ staid

12. teen superstar ......................... idol

13. green or black fruit ................... olive

14. former military person ................. vetran

15. reply .................................. answer

Answers on page 280

# Take Note

The grid below contains 16 kinds of music. Words may run forward or backward, up or down, or along diagonals, but they will always be in a straight line. When you've found all the words, read the leftover letters from left to right and top to bottom to learn why the hip-hop star went into the CD shop.

## Word list

Country
Disco
Funk
Golden oldie
Gospel
Hip-Hop
House
Jazz
Latin
Mood
Opera
Reggae
Rock
Soul
Swing
Techno

```
                          G
                          O   N
                          L       I
                          D           W
                          E               S
                          N               O   U
                          O               U   L
                          L               L
                          D               T

                  R   A   O   I
              O   M   P   R   E   H
          C   N   I   O   A   E   I   C
      K   K   H   U   G   O   S   P   E   L
      P   S   C   G   O   F   D   H   O   M
      E   R   E   S   U   O   H   O   A   P
      Y   R   T   N   U   O   C   P   Z   P
          I   K   N   G   S   P   Z   A
          P   N   I   T   A   L
          D   E   J   R
```

Answer _____

# Moving Around

Change each word into a different word by changing the order of the letters.

Example:　　　pea ⟶ ape

 1. not 　　　　　___ ___ ___

 2. tan 　　　　　___ ___ ___

 3. are 　　　　　___ ___ ___

 4. pit 　　　　　___ ___ ___

 5. left 　　　　　___ ___ ___ ___

 6. pale 　　　　　___ ___ ___ ___

 7. newt 　　　　　___ ___ ___ ___

 8. odor 　　　　　___ ___ ___ ___

 9. snake 　　　　　___ ___ ___ ___ ___

10. could 　　　　___ ___ ___ ___ ___

11. north 　　　　___ ___ ___ ___ ___

12. south 　　　　___ ___ ___ ___ ___

13. broad 　　　　___ ___ ___ ___ ___

14. shale 　　　　___ ___ ___ ___ ___

15. meats 　　　　___ ___ ___ ___ ___

16. stare 　　　　___ ___ ___ ___ ___

Answers on page 280

# Two Magic Squares

Magic word squares read the same both across and down. Answer the clues, and write them in the grid two times, once going across and once going down.

## Magic Square #1
Clues

1. Potato ___ (salty snack)
2. One who saves the day
3. Appliance used to get wrinkles out of clothes
4. Small horse

| 1 | 2 | 3 | 4 |
|---|---|---|---|
| 2 |   |   |   |
| 3 |   |   |   |
| 4 |   |   |   |

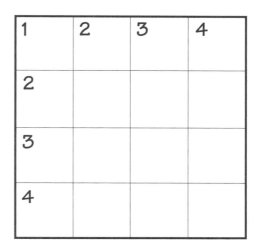

## Magic Square #2
Clues

1. It may twinkle in the night sky
2. "Dress" worn in ancient Rome
3. The Middle ___ (time period)
4. Itchy thing you might get from poison ivy

| 1 | 2 | 3 | 4 |
|---|---|---|---|
| 2 |   |   |   |
| 3 |   |   |   |
| 4 |   |   |   |

Answers on page 280

# Let's Get Together

Read each pair of clues, and write the answer for each clue. Then put the two answers together to form a new word.

1. _____kit_____ + _____ten_____ = _____kitten_____
   young beaver          one more than nine          a baby cat

2. _____ + _____ = _____
   motor vehicle          to decay          an orange vegetable

3. _____ + _____ = _____
   male person          to leave          a tropical fruit

4. _____ + _____ = _____
   past tense of "sit"          opposite of out          smooth, shiny fabric

5. _____ + _____ = _____
   "on the other hand"          2,000 pounds          a fastener for clothing

6. _____ + _____ = _____
   a tiny insect          folded edge of a garment          a national song

7. _____ + _____ = _____
   to steal          Indiana postal code          a songbird

8. _____ + _____ = _____
   place where ships dock          having ability          easily moved about

9. _____ + _____ = _____
   short for "professional"          an action word          a wise, old saying

10. _____ + _____ = _____
   type of smoked meat          to make fun of          a hanging net that serves as a bed

Answers on page 280

# Beam In on Bs

This picture is loaded with things that begin with the letter B. Finding 30 would be BEAUTIFUL. Finding more than 40 would be BRILLIANT indeed!

SCHOO

Answers on page 280

# Forward and Backward

A palindrome is a word that reads the same both forward and backward, such as *mom* or *tot*. Can you figure out the palindromes below?

1. pop      ___ ___ ___

2. soda      ___ ___ ___

3. cloth tied under a baby's chin      ___ ___ ___

4. what you see with      ___ ___ ___

5. past tense of "do"      ___ ___ ___

6. young dog      ___ ___ ___

7. a joke      ___ ___ ___

8. middle of the day      ___ ___ ___ ___

9. an exploit or a feat      ___ ___ ___ ___

10. flat and even      ___ ___ ___ ___ ___

11. a canoe with a small opening in the center

     ___ ___ ___ ___ ___

12. device for finding the location and position of a distant object ___ ___ ___ ___ ___

Answers on page 280

# Loony Limericks

A limerick is a humorous, five-line poem in which the first, second, and fifth lines rhyme and the third and fourth lines rhyme. Each line in these limericks ends with a jumbled word that you must unscramble to complete the poem. Both limericks end with a pun, which is a play on words. So we hope you'll have a lot of pun solving these puzzles.

1. The weatherman rarely was GIRTH,  _____

   So he said on the newscast one THING:  _____

   "I predict we'll see OWNS,  _____

   But I really don't WONK  _____

   If things will turn out all HEWIT."  _____

2. "Come look at this pony I DONUF!"  _____

   Said a girl to a boy who just WORDFEN.  _____

   He said, "Tell me the HURTT,  _____

   Is that really so, THRU,  _____

   Or are you just horsing NOURAD?"  _____

Answers on page 280

# Mountains of Fun

Vincent loves having fun in the snowy winter. Can you figure out what he likes to do? Connect the dots 1 through 101 to see Vincent up on his favorite mountain.

# Extreme Trivia Quiz

Each question comes with four possible answers.
Circle the correct answer.

1. Which of these famous people was born first?

Christopher Columbus    Cleopatra    George Washington    Hillary Clinton

2. Which of these things can travel the fastest?

Cheetah    Skateboard    Race car    Jet plane

3. Which of these countries has the most people?

United States    Brazil    China    Mexico

4. Which of these bodies in space is farthest from Earth?

Saturn    The moon    Mars    The sun

5. Which of these things weighs the most?

1,000 mosquitoes    10 sheets of paper    100 dimes    1 laptop computer

6. Which of these famous athletes walks the farthest
distance during a typical day of competition?

Lance Armstrong    Tom Brady    Tiger Woods    Roger Clemens

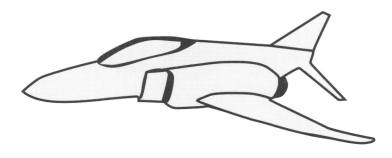

Answers on page 281

# The State of AEIOU

Someone has taken all the consonants and left only the vowels in the list of states below! Can you figure out the state names? We've done the first one for you.

1. I __ __ I A __ A     <u>INDIANA</u>

2. O __ E __ O __     _____

3. A __ A __ A __ A     _____

4. __ I __ __ I __ __ I __ __ I     _____

5. __ A __ I __ O __ __ I A     _____

6. __ E __ A __     _____

7. __ E __ __ E __ __ E E     _____

8. __ A I __ E     _____

9. __ E __ __ O __ __ (one word) _____

10. __ I __ __ I __ I A     _____

11. O __ __ A __ O __ A     _____

12. A __ I __ O __ A     _____

13. __ __ O __ I __ A     _____

14. __ E __ __ U __ __ __     _____

15. __ E O __ __ I A     _____

16. __ O __ __ E __ __ I __ U __     _____

17. I __ A __ O     _____

18. __ O __ __ A __ A     _____

19. __ E __ __ __ A __ __ A     _____

20. I __ __ I __ O I __     _____

Answers on page 281

# Bible Villains

These names of villains in the Bible are grouped together according to length. Place each name in the appropriate box. Continue until all the boxes are filled. Now that we put Judas Iscariot in for you—it's easy!

**4 Letters**
Ahab
Cain
Joab
Saul

**5 Letters**
Amnon
Annas
Balam
Haman
Herod
Jabin
~~Judas~~
Laban
Nabal
Satan

**6 Letters**
Abiram
Dathan
Sisera

**7 Letters**
Delilah
Goliath

**8 Letters**
Athaliah
~~Iscariot~~
Caiaphas
Manasseh

Answers on page 281

# Plurals

A noun that means more than one person, place, or thing is called *plural*. Write the plural of each noun on the line next to it.

1. Mouse _____

2. Man _____

3. Goose _____

4. Foot _____

5. Sheep _____

6. Leaf _____

7. Knife _____

8. Wolf _____

9. Calf _____

10. Deer _____

11. Woman _____

12. Elf _____

13. Scissors _____

14. Life _____

Answers on page 281

# Mix and Match Once Again

Rearrange the letters in each word on the left so you can add it to the word on the right to from a new word. (The first set is easy, but be prepared! It will get harder as you move along.)

1. GATES       _____COACH
2. TAXER       _____ORDINARY
3. LEAP       _____SURE
4. SHORE       _____SHOE
5. COATS       _____LINE

Now try a matching game!
Rearrange the letters in the numbered list to form a new word with one of the words on the right.

1. PEACH       _____ION
2. TRACE       _____FIELD
3. GRADER       _____MARE
4. THING       _____SKATE
5. TABLET       _____LESS

Now try the matching game in reverse!

1. _____TONE       FINDER
2. _____MIND       PURSE
3. _____SHEET       STREAM
4. _____MAN       SMILE
5. _____SHIP       DRAPES

Answers on page 281

# Here's the Scoop

Find 20 words and phrases about ice cream in the grid, which is shaped like an ice cream cone. Words will go across, up, down, and diagonal but always in a straight line. Circle the words as you find them in the grid, and cross them off the list. When you're done, read the uncircled letters in the grid from left to right, top to bottom, to spell out the answer to this riddle: What did the goofy magician say right before he ate his dessert?

## Word list

Butter pecan
Cherry
Chocolate
Cone
Creamy
Drip
Flavor
Frozen
Hot fudge sundae
Licks
Melt
Milk shake
Mint
Pint
Scoop
Soft
Sprinkles
Swirl
Toppings
Vanilla

```
            W A V T C
            C R E A M Y B
          H M P I N T E U R
          C O N E I E M T O
          O A Z H L K M T V
          C H O C O L A T E A K
          S E R M T T A H S R L Y I
          C F E S O F T S E P F T C
            R K P U E K L E A
            M C P D D L K C I
              I I G S I N A
              L N E A M I N
              P G S W I R L
                S U Y N P
                P N R T S
                E D R I P
                  A E A
                  E H R
                    C
```

Answer: _____

# Fivers

Ten words related to their topic are in the grids. To find them, pick one letter from each column going from left to right. Each letter in each grid will be used only once, so cross it off after you use it. We did the first one for you.

## Scary Halloween costumes

1. *GHOST*
2. _____
3. _____
4. _____
5. _____

| G | E | I | M | H |
|---|---|---|---|---|
| A | H | T | I | Y |
| W | U | O | E | L |
| D | I | M | S | N |
| M | L | V | C | T |

## Mammals

1. _____
2. _____
3. _____
4. _____
5. _____

| T | O | M | N | A |
|---|---|---|---|---|
| H | K | G | R | L |
| Z | A | R | E | E |
| C | I | B | S | R |
| S | E | U | E | K |

Answers on page 281

# Fun with Opposites

Fill in the blank spaces with a word that means the opposite of the word in parentheses. If you choose the correct word, the new word you form will have the meaning described in the brackets. We've done the first one for you.

1. (in)        POUTED              [sulked]

2. (wrong)     F _ _ _ _ _ E N      [scare]

3. (higher)    S _ _ _ _ _ _        [not as fast]

4. (out)       M U F F _ _          [breakfast food]

5. (young)     B _ _ _             [brave]

6. (close)     C _ _ _ _ H A G E N  [capital of Denmark]

7. (down)      P _ _ I L            [student]

8. (start)     F _ _ _ E R          [car part]

9. (cooked)    D _ _ _ E R          [part of a dresser]

10. (hate)     G _ _ _ _ S          [hand warmers]

11. (lose)     T _ _ _ E            [heavy string]

12. (push)     _ _ _ _ E T          [young chicken]

13. (slow)     B R E A K _ _ _ _    [morning meal]

14. (stood)    _ _ _ U R N          [sixth planet in the solar system]

15. (nothing)  H _ _ _ O W E E N    [October 31]

Answers on page 281

# Shake It Up

These crazy straws are all mixed up! Follow the straws to see which shake each kid is drinking from. (Warning: The straws sometimes cross—be careful to follow the right one!)

Answers on page 281

# Trading Places

Look at the words in each pair. Switch positions of a letter from each of the two words to create two new words that are related in some way.

Example:   dug ⟶ dog

pop ⟶ pup

1. bet ⟶ _____

cod ⟶ _____

2. mood ⟶ _____

feat ⟶ _____

3. dot ⟶ _____

peg ⟶ _____

4. rook ⟶ _____

bead ⟶ _____

5. trek ⟶ _____

bare ⟶ _____

6. hire ⟶ _____

feat ⟶ _____

7. stare ⟶ _____

shins ⟶ _____

8. bus ⟶ _____

yell ⟶ _____

9. had ⟶ _____

heat ⟶ _____

10. broad ⟶ _____

leaf ⟶ _____

Answers on page 281

# Age Puzzlers

Read the clues, and see if you can figure out
each person's age.

1. Kelcie's mom is 3 times older than Kelcie.
   Kelcie's grandmother is twice as old as Kelcie's mom.
   The sum of all three ages is 100.
   How old are Kelcie, her mom, and her grandmother?
   Kelcie _____                    Kelcie's mom _____
   Kelcie's grandmother _____

2. Jenny is 4 years older than Jamie.
   Jamie is 6 years older than Jan.
   Jan is 15. How old are Jenny and Jamie?
   Jenny _____                    Jamie _____

3. Peggy has a younger brother named Jimmy.
   The sum of Peggy's age and Jimmy's age is 30.
   The difference of their ages is 8.
   How old are Peggy and Jimmy?
   Peggy _____ Jimmy _____

4. Mandy's age is one half of Andy's age.
   Randy's age is one half of Mandy's age.
   The sum of their ages is 28.
   How old are Andy, Mandy, and Randy?
   Andy _____ Mandy _____ Randy _____

Answers on pages 281–282

# Heartbreaker Challenge

Connect the nine hearts by drawing only four lines—
without lifting your pencil!

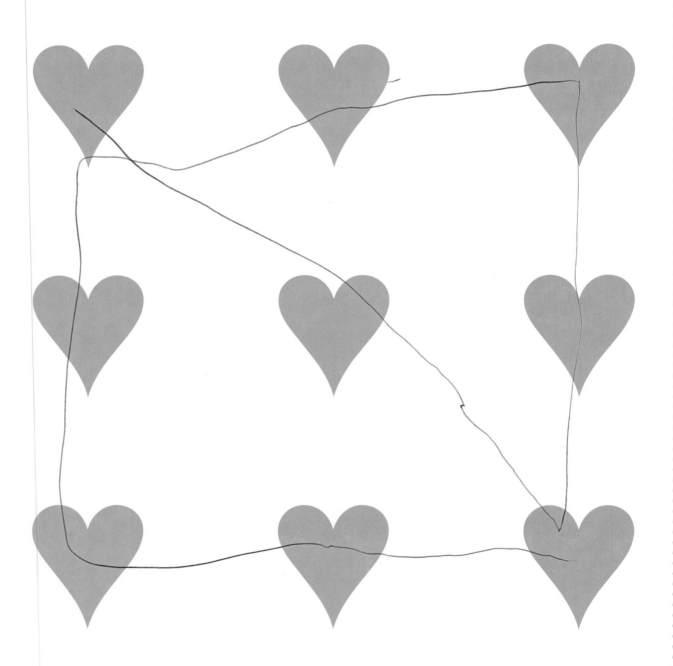

Answer on page 282

# Make-A-Word

Take one word from Column 1 plus one word from Column 2 plus one word from Column 3 to make a common word. Write the new word on the blank space. Be careful! Some words can be used with more than one other word. Each word should be used exactly once.

| Column 1 | Column 2 | Column 3 | Word |
|---|---|---|---|
| AM | A | ACHE | _____ |
| CAB | AD | AD | _____ |
| CAN | ART | AL | _____ |
| CAP | FOR | ATE | _____ |
| CAT | GET | BALL | _____ |
| DO | HE | HER | _____ |
| HE | I | LOG | _____ |
| IN | IT | MAT | _____ |
| ME | ON | MED | _____ |
| NO | OR | NET | _____ |
| RED | NON | OW | _____ |
| TO | PUT | TIME | _____ |

Answers on page 282

# Poetic License

Below is a list of words and phrases that might appear on a license plate. Use the clues in parentheses to help you figure out what they are.

1. YNOT    _____ (How come?)

2. CUSOON    _____ (Catch ya in the near future)

3. IH8U    _____ (You're awful!)

4. BLUEIII    _____ (Heavenly eyes)

5. PPPNCARROTS    _____ (Vegetables on a plate)

6. BALLTHATUCANB    _____ (Reach your potential)

7. YYYGUYS    _____ (Smart alecks)

8. MAKINGNMEEE    _____ (Creating foes)

9. RUUP4IT    _____ (Ready to take a chance?)

10. ILBBACK    _____ (Famous last words)

Answers on page 282

# A Lark in the Park

There are 15 differences between the top and the bottom park scene. Can you spot all of them?

Answers on page 282

# Word Ladders

Change just one letter on each line to go from the top word to the bottom word. Use the clues to guide you.

1.    GIVE          Donate (to)
    \_\_ \_\_ \_\_ \_\_     Bee's home
    \_\_ \_\_ \_\_ \_\_     Go up a mountain trail
    \_\_ \_\_ \_\_ \_\_     Two-wheeler
    \_\_ \_\_ \_\_ \_\_     Use the oven
    TAKE          Capture

2.    PASS          Succeed on a test at school
    \_\_ \_\_ \_\_ \_\_     Dog's feet
    \_\_ \_\_ \_\_ \_\_     Chess piece
    \_\_ \_\_ \_\_ \_\_     Sharp ache
    \_\_ \_\_ \_\_ \_\_     What Jack and Jill went to get
    FAIL          Flunk a test

3.    WORK         What one does at an office
    \_\_ \_\_ \_\_ \_\_     Plug for a bottle
    \_\_ \_\_ \_\_ \_\_     Make a hot dinner
    \_\_ \_\_ \_\_ \_\_     Hen house
    \_\_ \_\_ \_\_ \_\_     Sound of a horse's hoof on pavement
    \_\_ \_\_ \_\_ \_\_     Applaud
    \_\_ \_\_ \_\_ \_\_     Material to mold in kindergarten
    PLAY          Recreation

4.    HAND         It's at the end of an arm
    \_\_ \_\_ \_\_ \_\_     Magician's stick
    \_\_ \_\_ \_\_ \_\_     Wish to have
    \_\_ \_\_ \_\_ \_\_     Blemish, perhaps on a witch
    \_\_ \_\_ \_\_ \_\_     Opposite of cool
    \_\_ \_\_ \_\_ \_\_     Place to grow crops
    \_\_ \_\_ \_\_ \_\_     Shape
    \_\_ \_\_ \_\_ \_\_     Where the cavalry may be stationed
    FOOT          It's at the end of a leg

Answers on page 282

# Word Pyramids

Use the clues in parentheses to fill in the missing words in these pyramids. Each level builds on the last one—just add one letter to the previous word and rearrange the letters as necessary.

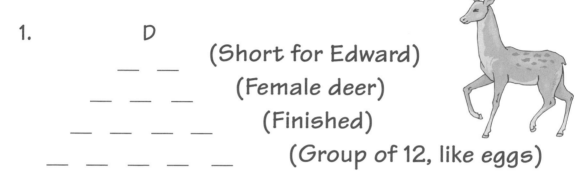

1.      D
     __ __          (Short for Edward)
   __ __ __         (Female deer)
 __ __ __ __        (Finished)
__ __ __ __ __      (Group of 12, like eggs)


2.          S
     __ __          ("Who ___ it?")
   __ __ __         (Use a chair)
 __ __ __ __        (Father's Day gifts)
__ __ __ __ __      (Ways to get out of a theater)


3.          A
     __ __          ("What ___ I to do?")
   __ __ __         (Charge into)
 __ __ __ __        (Fighting troops)
__ __ __ __ __      (Leader of a city)

Answers on page 282

# Ships Ahoy!

Arrange the ship-related words in alphabetical order, and write them in the boxes. Then read down the shaded column to find the answer to this riddle:

Riddle: What kind of fruit do you find on ships?

schooner

tanker

saltwater

anchor

navigate

porthole

captain

vessel

shipping

ocean

rudder

propeller

Answer:_____

# Squished Countries

Two foreign countries have been squished together on each line. All the letters of both countries are in the correct order; you just have to separate them. You will use each letter exactly once. The first one has been done for you.

1. B R P O A Z L A I L N D      <u>BRAZIL/POLAND</u>

2. G R L E B E E A N C E O N      _____

3. A U S C U T R A L B A I A      _____

4. T U V I E R K E T N Y A M      _____

5. V E N S W I T E Z U E Z E R L A N D L A      _____

6. S N O R I N G A P O W A R E Y      _____

7. A F G H B O L A N I S I V I A T A N      _____

8. B E G E R L G I M A U M N Y      _____

9. R E U G S Y S P I T A      _____

10. I H N D I O N D A U R A S      _____

Answers on pages 282–283

# Selections

The words on each line look similar, but only one has the
same meaning as the definition in parentheses.
Select the correct word, and circle it.
It's also okay to use a dictionary!

1. CONTRIVE     CONTROL     CONTOUR     (have power over)

2. DELECTABLE     DELEGATE     DELETED     (got rid of)

3. EMPLOYEE     EMPLOYER     EMPOWER     (worker)

4. INFURIATE     INFORMAL     INFORM     (casual)

5. INTRUDES     INTERNS     INVESTS     (comes in without being asked)

6. IVY     ISLE     IVORY     (creamy white color)

7. OVERWHELM     OVERTURE     OVERTIME     (beginning music)

8. PERMANENT     PERMEATE     PERMISSION     (lasting)

9. QUARRELED     QUARTERED     QUALIFIED     (argued)

10. SCARFACE     SCANDAL     SCAFFOLD     (platform for construction workers)

11. THRUST     THRASH     THRIVE     (develop successfully)

12. VENERATE     VERTEBRATE     VENTILATE     (supply fresh air to)

Answers on page 283

# Hidden Meanings

Write the word or phrase that matches each clue below.

| | | |
|---|---|---|
| 1.    R<br>ROAD<br>A<br>D<br><br>_____ | 2.    CENTURY<br><br>_____ | 3.    PAINS<br><br>_____ |
| 4.    WEAR<br>     LONG<br><br>_____<br>_____ | 5.<br><br>    POX<br><br>_____ | 6.<br><br>GEGS   EGSG<br><br>_____ |
| 7.<br><br>meQUIT<br><br>_____<br>_____ | 8.   HOUR<br><br>_____ | 9.    C<br>     UNDER<br><br>_____ |
| 10.    T<br>     O<br>     W<br>     N<br><br>_____ | 11.<br>    LEFT<br>    PIZZA<br><br>_____ | 12.    K<br>     C<br>     E<br>     H<br>     C<br><br>_____ |

Answers on page 283

# Unfinished Food

A three-letter word has been removed from each food word shown here. Take a word from the Word list, and put it into the blank spaces on a line to make a food. Cross off each word as you use it.

Word list

Cab
Hip
How
Ice
Lad
Let
Mud
Par
Pop
Rap
Row
Run
Sag
Tar
Tea

1. G __ __ __ E
2. P __ __ __ E
3. __ __ __ B A G E
4. B E R __ __ __ A   O N I O N
5. W __ __ __ P E D   C R E A M
6. N E C __ __ __ I N E
7. S __ __ __ E   R I B S
8. S __ __ __ K
9. L A __ __ __ N A
10. T U N A   F I S H   S A __ __ __
11. B __ __ __ N I E
12. C L A M   C __ __ __ D E R
13. V E A L   C U T __ __ __
14. F R I E D   R __ __ __
15. __ __ __ C O R N

Answers on page 283

# Yummy Partners

In each puzzle, the names of two foods have been mixed together. Take out one food to find the other.

Example:   mpoetaattoes   =   meat and potatoes

1. coomkiilkes = _____ and _____

2. aporpangleess = _____ and _____

3. crcachekeersse = _____ and _____

4. llemimoen = _____ and _____

5. tjoaasmt = _____ and _____

6. ssoaluapd = _____ and _____

7. hfamrbuirgeers = _____ and _____

8. spamegathebaltltis = _____ and _____

9. beagcgons = _____ and _____

10. pasnycraukeps = _____ and _____

Answers on page 283

# Wacky Wordies

Each set of words is a wacky way to show a common phrase. Study each set, and try to solve the riddle.

1. RED RIDING HOOD  _____

2.  GOING
   VACATION  _____

3. COORDERURT  _____

4. IT'S NO **DEAL**  _____

5. I KNOW A CUT  _____

6. O ● NE  _____

Answers on page 283

# Word Magic

Change *book* to *fork*. Change only one letter at a time. Use the picture clues to help you.

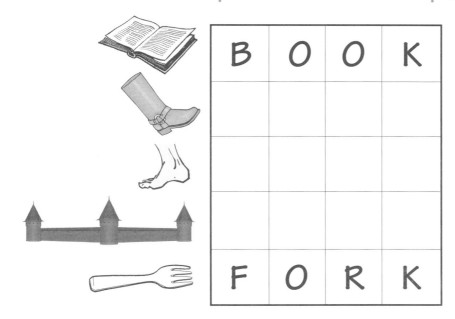

| B | O | O | K |
|---|---|---|---|
|   |   |   |   |
|   |   |   |   |
|   |   |   |   |
| F | O | R | K |

Now change *page* to *bone*.

| P | A | G | E |
|---|---|---|---|
|   |   |   |   |
|   |   |   |   |
|   |   |   |   |
| B | O | N | E |

Now change *well* to *band*.

| W | E | L | L |
|---|---|---|---|
|   |   |   |   |
|   |   |   |   |
|   |   |   |   |
| B | A | N | D |

Answers on page 283

# Yes and No

Use the clues to help you discover words
that contain yes or no.

1. what you see with — __ yes

2. the most bashful — __ __ yes __

3. the day before today — yes __ __ __ __ __ __

4. the most crafty or cunning — __ __ yes __

5. the ability to see — __ yes __ __ __

6. substances used to change
   the color of something — __ yes

7. a short letter or message — no __ __

8. a direction on a compass — no __ __ __

9. flakes of ice that fall from the sky — __ no __

10. a sound — no __ __ __

11. to bang or hit, especially on a door — __ no __ __

12. a narrow boat — __ __ no __

13. a heavy gun that fires metal balls — __ __ __ no __

14. the kind of writing that is about
    real people, things, and events — no __ __ __ __ __ __ __ __ __

Answers on page 283

# Famous Men in the Bible

Fill in the answers to the clues by using all the syllables in the box. The number of syllables to be used in each answer is shown in brackets. Place one letter in each blank. Each syllable in the box will be used just once.

| A AD AH AM BAR BAS BRA DA DAS DE HAM JU |
| MO MON MUS NA NIC NO O O PE SES SOL TER VID |

1. He feared the rooster crow     [2] _ _ _ _ _ _

2. God gave him wisdom     [3] _ _ _ _ _ _ _ _

3. First man     [2] _ _ _ _ _

4. Jesus' Pharisee friend     [4] _ _ _ _ _ _ _ _ _ _

5. Father of Jews and Arabs     [3] _ _ _ _ _ _ _ _

6. He built the ark     [2] _ _ _ _

7. He betrayed Jesus for money     [2] _ _ _ _ _ _

8. Known as the "Lawgiver"     [2] _ _ _ _ _

9. This shepherd killed Goliath     [2] _ _ _ _ _

10. Paul's companion     [3] _ _ _ _ _ _ _ _ _

Answers on page 283

# Crossword

1. Sticky stuff used on roads
4. Jack-in-____-box
7. A violin player uses one
10. "Hurray," in a bullfight
11. "Mary ____ a little lamb"
12. Have debts
13. He "was a merry old soul": 3 words
16. Finished
17. Attack like a bee
20. Made stitches
24. Electric ____ (kind of fish)
25. "____ Been Working on the Railroad"
26. Stories
29. Single square of a comic strip
31. Capital of Oregon
33. He "met a pieman": 2 words
39. The highest card in many games
40. Explosive stuff
41. Number of wheels on a unicycle
42. Sopping ____
43. Letters that mean "help!"
44. A dog's hand

DOWN

1. Also
2. "____ aboard!"
3. A color on the American flag
4. Item
5. You might raise it in class
6. Sides
7. Ghostly noise
8. Bird that hoots
9. ____ Willie Winkie
14. Barbie's ex-boyfriend
15. Letters between B and F
17. All ____ (ready to go)
18. Drink that's made from leaves
19. Unhealthy
21. Opposite of lose
22. Adam's wife

23. Dover's state: Abbreviation
27. The "sixth sense": Abbreviation
28. Sprinkles with a white seasoning
29. Annoying little bugs
30. "What a good boy ___!" (what Little Jack Horner said): 2 words

32. Jay ___ (late-night talk show host)
33. Cutting tool
34. It cools down a drink
35. "Have we ___ somewhere before?"
36. It can clean a floor
37. Go ___ wild-goose chase: 2 words
38. ___ Mexico (state)

| 1 | 2 | 3 | | 4 | 5 | 6 | | 7 | 8 | 9 |
|---|---|---|---|---|---|---|---|---|---|---|
| 10 | | | | 11 | | | | 12 | | |
| 13 | | | 14 | | | 15 | | | | |
| | | | 16 | | | | | | | |
| 17 | 18 | 19 | | | 20 | | 21 | 22 | 23 | |
| 24 | | | | | | | 25 | | | |
| 26 | | | 27 | 28 | | 29 | 30 | | | |
| | | | 31 | | 32 | | | | | |
| 33 | 34 | 35 | | | | | 36 | 37 | 38 | |
| 39 | | | | 40 | | | 41 | | | |
| 42 | | | | 43 | | | 44 | | | |

Answers on page 283

# On Top of Spaghetti

... all covered with cheese. The mouse lost his meatball when somebody sneezed. Help him get to it!

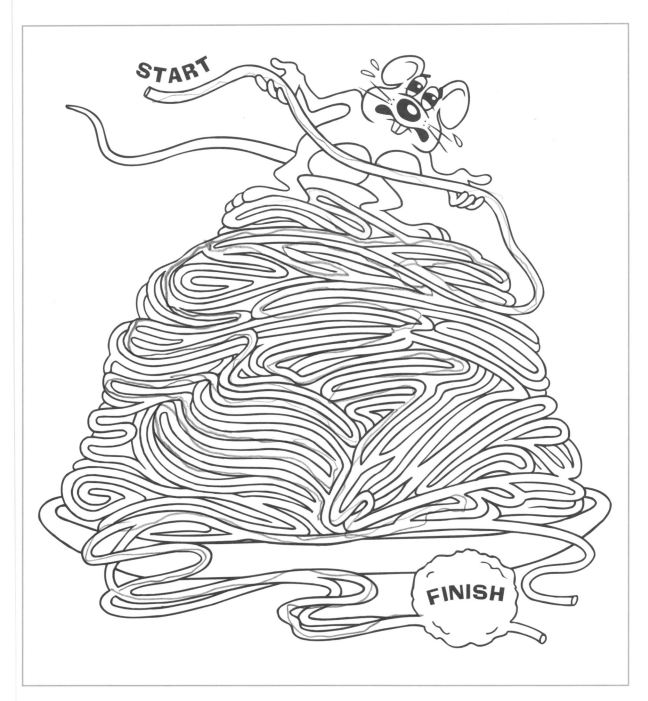

Answer on page 283

# Rhyme Time

It's time to rhyme. In this word search, do NOT look in the grid for the words in the list below. Instead, look for words that rhyme with them. For example, WRITE is listed, but BRIGHT is in the grid. (We've circled it for you.) As you find a word in the grid, circle it and write it on the blank line next to its rhyme. Words in the grid will run straight across, backward, up, down, or diagonal but always in a straight line. Two hints: The answers in the list are in alphabetical order, and no two hidden words begin with the same letter.

1. Write _____BRIGHT_____

2. Hassle _____

3. School _____

4. Down _____

5. Cavity _____

6. Grandstand _____

7. Hockey _____

8. True _____

9. After _____

10. Fixed _____

11. Eyes _____

12. Fried _____

13. Tallest _____

14. Dirty _____

15. Hiking _____

16. Aisle _____

```
L H S N P G B O J O
O A T H I R T Y O Z
O N U W I A I E C T
R D B G H V R Z K S
D S H E H I W S E E
C T C A S T L E Y L
K A L R U Y E E E L
G N I K I V S R A A
N D E D Z D E X I M
F R O W N O E O S S
```

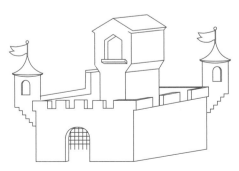

Answers on page 283

# Going for the Green

All the words in the word list are things that are green. Find these words in the leaf-shaped grid as you look across, down, and diagonally. Circle each word as you find it, and cross it off the word list.

## Word list

Algae
Avocado
Broccoli
Cactus
Grape
Grass
Grinch
Incredible Hulk
Jade
Kermit the Frog
Leaf
Mint
Moss
Peas
Pickle
Pine
Poison Ivy
Slime
Spinach
Turtles

```
                    B
                 S  R  S
              H  L  O  A  M
           R  P  I  C  K  L  E
           O  K  M  C  C  A  P
        K  S  E  E  O  G  D  A  G
        T  U  R  T  L  E  S  R  O
        L  A  M  A  I  L  A  G  S
        Y  V  I  N  O  S  I  O  P
        A  O  T  R  S  P  J  E  I
        B  C  T  I  I  L  A  S  N
        L  A  H  N  N  S  D  U  A
        S  D  E  P  C  E  E  T  C
        S  O  F  G  R  I  N  C  H
           S  R  L  E  A  F  A
           T  O  E  D  R  P  C
           G  M  I  N  T
           A  B  N
              L
              E
              H
              U
              L
              K
```

Answers on page 284

# Letter Perfect

Fill in the blanks with letters that form the word described in parentheses.

1. __ __ __ L E T __          (sporty person)
2. __ __ __ L E T          (artistic form of dancing)
3. __ __ __ __ L E T          (pamphlet)
4. __ __ __ __ __ L E T          (jewelry worn on the wrist)
5. L E T __ __ __ __          (main salad ingredient)
6. __ __ __ __ L E T __ __          (plant clipping used as a Christmas decoration)
7. __ __ __ L E T          (egg dish popular at brunch)
8. __ __ __ __ L E T          (shade of red)
9. __ __ __ L E T __ __          (set of bones that supports the body)
10. __ __ __ __ L E T          (frying pan)
11. __ __ __ __ L E T __          (three siblings born at the same time)
12. __ __ __ L E T          (purple spring flower)
13. __ __ __ L E T          (money holder)

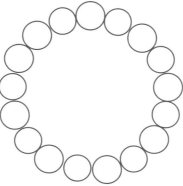

Answers on page 284

# You're Precious

Search for the treasure trove of 21 words and phrases about gems and jewelry in the grid below. Words may run forward or backward, up or down, or along diagonals, but they are always in a straight line. When you've found all the words, read the uncircled letters from left to right and top to bottom to answer the riddle: When shopping for jewelry, why did the confused bellydancer seek out a group of sailors?

**Word list**

| | | |
|---|---|---|
| Bangle | Emerald | Quartz |
| Beryl | Garnet | Ruby |
| Bracelet | Gemstone | Sapphire |
| Cameo | Locket | Tiara |
| Charm | Necklace | Topaz |
| Diamond | Opal | Turquoise |
| Earring | Pearl | |
| | Pendant | |

```
        G L E R I H P P A S L
      S A H M E W T P A D Y Y S
    L P R O E O O E K I B T R N I
  N O G N B R P A A A U N F E O R Q
  T E L E C A R B M R A H C B G U A
  U T T Z L N O N D A K A N A G
  R E V D N G N A L I I R E
    Q K D L E L A R R T M
      U C P I C E R Z S
      O O E M A C T
        I L E N O
        S G N
        E
```

# Add Another Word

Each of the following four words can have the same three-letter word added to its beginning to make new words. Find that three-letter word.

_____ on
_____ bell
_____ king
_____ red

Find another three-letter word to go with these four words.

_____ arctic
_____ hem
_____ elope
_____ acid

Now here's a really hard one to find.

_____ size
_____ able
_____ rice
_____ stone

Answers on page 284

# Start at the End

On each line, put the same three letters in both sets of empty spaces to form the end of the first word and the beginning of the second word. Use the clues in parentheses to guide you for the first word and the clues in brackets to help you with the second word. The three letters you add will be a common word.

1. (colorful arc) RAIN _ _ _/_ _ _ LING [game with lanes]

2. (take place) HAP _ _ _/_ _ _ CIL [writing tool]

3. (throwing weapon) SP _ _ _/_ _ _ RING [jewelry]

4. (circle in space) OR _ _ _/_ _ _ TEN [chomped on]

5. (smelled) WHIF _ _ _/_ _ _ ERAL [type of government]

6. (Thanksgiving pie) PUMP _ _ _/_ _ _ DLY [nice]

7. (evening sky) SUN _ _ _/_ _ _ TLER [pioneer]

8. (hot drink holder) TEA _ _ _/_ _ _ ID [arrow shooter]

9. (Valentine shape) HE _ _ _/_ _ _ ICLE [magazine story]

10. (chess piece) BIS _ _ _/_ _ _ EFUL [optimistic]

11. (book of listings) CATA _ _ _/_ _ _ ICAL [reasonable]

12. (camel train) CARA _ _ _/_ _ _ ISH [disappear]

Answers on page 284

# Amusement Park

You won't need a ticket to visit this wacky amusement park! Test your powers of observation by completing the following activities. Don't use the same answer twice.

1. Find 5 things that don't belong in an amusement park.
2. Find 5 things that begin with the letter R.
3. Find 3 things hidden in this picture.

Answers on page 284

# Scrambled Synonyms

Unscramble both words on each line to find a pair of similar words. The words can be nouns, verbs, or adjectives. For example, *IDSH & LAPET* would be *DISH & PLATE*.

1. EADWOM & LIFDE _____

2. STUGE & ISVIROT _____

3. SARTH & BAGRAGE _____

4. LOCD & HYLICL _____

5. NARI & UPRO _____

6. ANET & DIYT _____

7. RITDY & LIFTYH _____

8. THOSU & CARMES _____

9. TARMS & LERVEC _____

10. RETPYT & UTEC _____

11. DAYL & NOMAW _____

12. TERRWI & ROTHUA _____

Answers on page 284

# Measuring Up

Place the various types of measurements below into the diagram so that they interlock as in a crossword. When you are done, all the words will have been used exactly once.

**3 Letters**
Cup
Day
Ton

**4 Letters**
Acre
Byte
Mile
Peck
Week
Yard
Year

**5 Letters**
Carat
Liter
Meter
Month
Ounce
Pound
Quart

**6 Letters**
Barrel
Gallon
Second

**7 Letters**
Calorie

**9 Letters**
Centigram

**10 Letters**
Horsepower

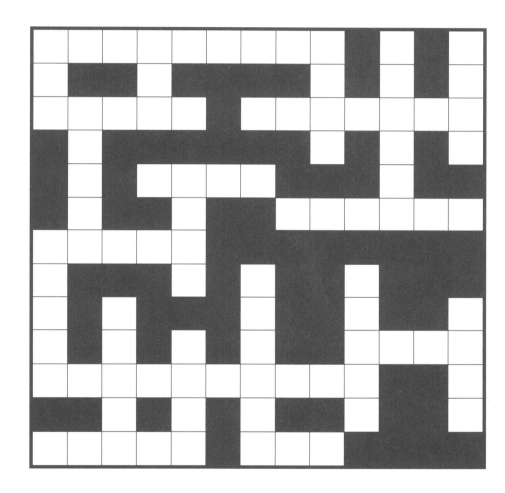

Answers on page 284

217

# Eye Rhymes

Words that have the same endings often rhyme—but sometimes they don't. For example, the word *BUSH* rhymes with *PUSH* but not with *RUSH*. For each word listed, change the first letter to come up with another word that looks like it should rhyme but doesn't. For numbers 11 and 12, come up with two new words that also don't rhyme with each other. We've done the first one for you.

1. CAR      *WAR*

2. CATCH      _____

3. WAVE      _____

4. CASH      _____

5. NORTH      _____

6. WOLF      _____

7. BLOW      _____

8. HEIGHT      _____

9. WORSE      _____

10. LEASE      _____

11. BONE      _____ & _____

12. HOSE      _____ & _____

Answers on page 284

# Find-a-President

Circle the last names of 14 U.S. presidents hidden in the sentences below. Three pairs of presidents have the same last name. The first one is done for you.

1. If I take the (bus, h)ow long will it take to get to the White House?

2. I am aware a gander followed a goose and ended up at the farm.

3. Should we do the washing tonight or tomorrow?

4. Pirates sent rum and gold home to their families.

5. What makes John so nervous?

6. I'm glad Amsterdam's tulips are blooming early.

7. Take the car, Terry, and I'll meet you there.

8. In Soho, over the lake flew the wild geese.

9. That kind of pool is sunken, Ned. You can't put it above ground.

10. Clint only eats the Idaho potatoes his father grows.

11. Times are hard in ghost towns.

Answers on page 284

# Crossword

## ACROSS

1. Cash machine at a bank: Abbreviation
4. Paintings
7. Hot-chocolate holder
10. Be in debt
11. Sheep sound
12. High ___ kite: 2 words
13. What a 33-Across has: 3 words
16. Go into a building
17. Home base in baseball
20. Car fender flaws
24. Fast plane
25. Word from a ghost
26. Parts of a stairway
29. Like bath water while washing
31. Place in a church where people marry
33. Very wealthy person
39. Do it ___ dare: 2 words
40. Angry
41. Twenty-four hours
42. What a dog does with its tail
43. Football game gains: Abbreviation
44. Half of 2-Down

## DOWN

1. Dial-up service for getting to the Internet: Abbreviation
2. Half of four
3. Was introduced to someone
4. Something to give the dog to chew on: 2 words
5. Inflatable thing to lie on in a pool
6. Made less wild
7. Is able to
8. Take advantage of
9. Salary from a job
14. Get the table ready for dinner
15. State north of California: Abbreviation
17. Child's sleeping clothes, for short
18. Allow
19. Had dinner
21. League for the Lakers and Pistons

22. Spinning toy
23. Type of bean or milk
27. Buddy
28. Oozy and yucky
29. Beach materials
30. "Are you a man ___ mouse?": 2 words
32. Frog's cousin

33. Cut the grass
34. "...partridge ___ pear tree": 2 words
35. Fall behind
36. Words said during a wedding: 2 words
37. Sprinted
38. It sounds like "I"

| 1 | 2 | 3 | | 4 | 5 | 6 | | 7 | 8 | 9 |
|---|---|---|---|---|---|---|---|---|---|---|
| 10 | | | | 11 | | | | 12 | | |
| 13 | | | 14 | | | | 15 | | | |
| | | | 16 | | | | | | | |
| 17 | 18 | 19 | | | | 20 | | 21 | 22 | 23 |
| 24 | | | | | | | | 25 | | |
| 26 | | | 27 | 28 | | 29 | 30 | | | |
| | | | 31 | | 32 | | | | | |
| 33 | 34 | 35 | | | | | | 36 | 37 | 38 |
| 39 | | | | 40 | | | | 41 | | |
| 42 | | | | 43 | | | | 44 | | |

Answers on page 285

# Wild Wally's Waterpark

Jump on an inner tube, and slide through the maze to the tropical lagoon.

Answer on page 285

# Going Ape

Fill in the blanks to form the answer
to each clue.

1. _ _ A P E _            (small church)

2. _ _ A P E _            (window coverings)

3. _ _ A P E _            (circles, squares, triangles)

4. _ _ _ _ _ _ A P E        (a painting of woods, farms, etc.)

5. _ _ A P E _            (small green or red fruits)

6. _ A P E _             (part of a jacket or coat)

7. _ _ _ A P E           (knee or elbow abrasion)

8. _ _ A P E _            (piled)

9. _ _ A P E _            (brought in the crops)

10. _ A P E _            (used a VCR)

11. _ _ _ A P E          (get out of prison illegally)

12. _ A P E _            (writing material)

Answers on page 285

# Fivers

Five 5-letter drinks are hidden in the first mini grid below. To find them, use one letter from each column going from left to right. Each letter will be used once, so circle each one after you use it. The first word has been done for you.

## DRINKS

1. _WATER_
2. _____
3. _____
4. _____
5. _____

| W | O | T | E | H |
|---|---|---|---|---|
| P | U | C | C | A |
| C | A | D | O | R |
| J | I | N | C | E |
| C | U | I | E | R |

In the second grid there are five 5-letter fruits to be found. Again, use one letter from each column going from left to right.

## FRUITS

1. _____
2. _____
3. _____
4. _____
5. _____

| A | E | A | O | E |
|---|---|---|---|---|
| G | P | L | P | N |
| L | E | P | R | Y |
| M | R | M | L | N |
| B | E | R | O | E |

Answers on page 285

# Partials

On each line, put the same two letters in both empty spaces to form the end of the first word and the beginning of the second word. Use the clues in parentheses to guide you for the first word and the clues in brackets to help you with the second word.

1. (form of wrestling)   J U __ __ / __ __ U G H   [slang for money]

2. (get there)   A R R I __ __ / __ __ N O M   [a snake's poison]

3. (break into bits)   S M A __ __ / __ __ E L F   [ledge]

4. (hard experience)   O R D E __ __ / __ __ I K E   [similar]

5. (light rain)   D R I Z Z __ __ / __ __ O P A R D   [wild cat]

6. (rough drawing)   S K E T __ __ / __ __ O O S E   [select]

7. (formal argument)   D E B A __ __ / __ __ R R I F Y   [frighten]

8. (attractive)   P R E T __ __ / __ __ P H O O N   [hurricane]

9. (be in charge)   M A N A __ __ / __ __ N E R A L   [army officer]

10. (awful)   H O R R __ __ / __ __ E A L   [perfect]

11. ("laughing" animal)   H Y E __ __ / __ __ T U R A L   [not artificial]

12. (cutting utensil)   K N I __ __ / __ __ E B L E   [weak]

Answers on page 285

# Crisscross Connection

The words that go into the three crisscrosses below have been combined onto one word list. The subjects are Fabrics, Tools, and Languages. Cross out each word after you place it.

**Fabrics**

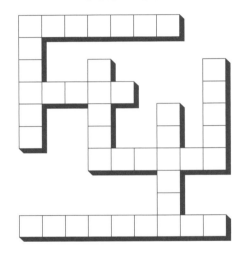

**3 Letters**
Saw

**5 Letters**
Czech
Denim
Drill
Latin
Level
Linen
Satin

**Languages**

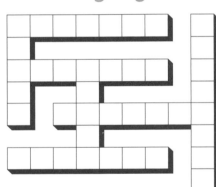

**6 Letters**
Burlap
Hammer
Muslin
Pliers
Sander
Velvet
Wrench

Spanish
Stapler

**Tools**

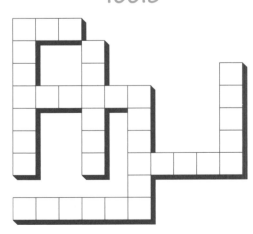

**8 Letters**
Japanese

**7 Letters**
Brocade
Chinese
English
Italian

**9 Letters**
Polyester

Answers on page 285

# Fun with Idioms

An idiom is an expression that means something other than what the words actually say. For example, "to let the cat out of the bag" means to give away a secret. Use the picture clues to help you complete the idioms below.

1. I think about Lee all the time. Lee is the _____ of my eye.

2. Even though Matt was busy, he would have gone to the concert at the drop of a _____.

3. Jerry is the _____ _____ of his family. He didn't go into the family business like his brothers.

4. Lisa is so happy! She's sitting on top of the _____ right now.

5. Craig gets _____ in his stomach whenever he has to fly.

6. I saved all year for a car, but I still only have a drop in the _____.

7. Patti loved math, so she thought the math test was a piece of _____.

8. When Dad saw the telephone bill, he hit the _____.

9. Laura was so annoyed when Bill kept asking to copy her homework that she finally told him to go fly a _____.

10. Since you have a big test tomorrow, you better hit the _____.

11. Bert was so uncomfortable at the party, he felt like a _____ out of water.

12. I usually don't like to watch TV, but once in a blue _____ there's something worth seeing.

Answers on page 285

# Number Squares

Put each number from 1 to 9 in the grid so that every row and every column adds up to 15. Every number will be used exactly once. We've placed 1, 4, 7, and 9 for you.

1.

| 9 | 4 |   |
|---|---|---|
|   |   | 7 |
| 1 |   |   |

Place each number from 0 to 8 in the grid so that every row and column adds up to 12. Every number will be used exactly once. This time we've placed only three numbers for you: 0, 6, and 7.

2.

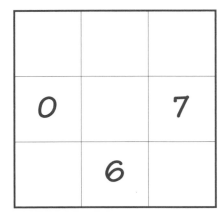

|   |   |   |
|---|---|---|
| 0 |   | 7 |
|   | 6 |   |

Answers on page 285

# Number Challenge

Fill in this crossword with numbers instead of letters. Start with 1-Across, a simple multiplication problem (which you can probably do in your head). Using a calculator or just your brain, figure out the answers to the rest of the Across clues. Then you can tackle the Down clues.

## Across

1. 5 x 5
3. 1-Across plus 100
6. 1-Across minus 4
7. 3-Across times 6-Across
8. 7-Across minus 600
10. 6-Across times 2
11. 3-Across plus 199
13. 2 more than 10-Across
15. 13-Across x 13-Across
18. 8-Across minus 3
20. 6-Across times 3
21. 11-Across minus 75
22. 20-Across plus 4

## Down

1. 21-Across minus 27
2. 1-Down plus 288
3. 6-Across minus 5
4. 2 more than 1-Down
5. 2-Down plus 42
7. 7-Across times 9 plus 1587
9. 2 more than 6-Across
12. 3-Down plus 33
13. 1-Down plus 200
14. 13-Down minus 18
16. 14-Down minus 38
17. 5-Down plus 85
19. 9-Down plus 6

Answers on page 285

# Body Language

Write the words that match the meanings below. Each answer is a compound word formed by combining the name of a body part with another word.

1. A bag or purse for carrying small items  ＿＿＿＿＿＿＿＿

2. An oval ball that is kicked during play  ＿＿＿＿＿＿＿＿

3. A mark left on an object after you hold it  ＿＿＿＿＿＿＿＿＿＿

4. A small timepiece that you wear  ＿＿＿＿＿＿＿

5. A device for listening to music  ＿＿＿＿＿＿＿＿

6. A pair of plastic lenses mounted on frames to correct poor vision  ＿＿＿＿＿＿＿

7. A small colored cosmetic used to tint a woman's mouth  ＿＿＿＿＿＿＿＿

8. A long, narrow strip of fabric that is worn under a shirt collar  ＿＿＿＿＿＿

9. A bright electrical unit on the front of a car  ＿＿＿＿＿＿＿＿＿

10. The part of a musical instrument that is placed between the lips  ＿＿＿＿＿＿＿＿＿

11. A comfortable seat with sides on it  ＿＿＿＿＿＿＿

12. A large bag that students use for carrying books  ＿＿＿＿＿＿＿

Answers on page 286

# Whose Flag Is That?

Read the clues to help you determine which country each flag represents.

 1. Nation just north of the United States

_____

 2. Nation just south of the United States

_____

 3. Home of the Great Wall

_____

 4. A country that lies in both Europe and Asia

_____

 5. The largest country in South America

_____

 6. The land known as "down under"

_____

 7. An Asian country known as "the land of the rising sun"

_____

 8. An African country founded by freed American slaves

_____

Answers on page 286

# Relations

Change one letter in each word to find three items that are related. For example, ROD, WHINE, and CLUE would become RED, WHITE, and BLUE. Write these new words on the lines next to the words. Then write what the items have in common on the longer line. In our example, all three words are colors of the U.S. flag.

1. MILE _____
   TOFFEE _____
   TEN _____

   _____

2. STORK _____
   BOOT _____
   POET _____

   _____

3. WAR _____
   BUN _____
   VAT _____

   _____

4. CORK _____
   BEAK _____
   PARROT _____

   _____

5. BARN _____
   VISA _____
   HOMES _____

   _____

6. MATCH _____
   JUNK _____
   JURY _____

   _____

7. CHAIN _____
   BELCH _____
   SODA _____

   _____

8. SPACE _____
   HEARS _____
   FLUB _____

   _____

9. LOUSE _____
   MODEL _____
   PRINTED _____

   _____

10. PARTS _____
    ROSE _____
    MERLIN _____

    _____

Answers on page 286

# Crossword

## ACROSS

1. Dog who barks at the moon
6. Take ___ (nod to the audience after performing): 2 words
10. "___ to go" (you say it when you need to leave): 2 words
11. Full of rocks
12. Starchy food often served with a steak: 2 words
14. Finished
15. Another way to prepare that starchy food in 12-Across
19. Alphabet letters after L
23. Movie star
24. Big stage production with music, like *Aida*
25. Loch ___ (lake with a monster)
26. Something to melt on top of 12-Across
27. Get ___ on the back (get approval): 2 words

29. Starchy food often served with a burger: 2 words
36. Last name of Homer Simpson's boss
37. "___ tired" (it may said when you're exhausted): 3 words
38. "___ miracle!" ("Holy cow!"): 2 words
39. Uses a computer keyboard

## DOWN

1. What a baby wears if it's a messy eater
2. "I get it now!"
3. Talk on and on
4. Woman in the Garden of Eden
5. More beet-colored
6. Try
7. ___ constrictor (snake)
8. Toronto's province: Abbreviation
9. Cheyenne is the capital of this state: Abbreviation
11. Male child

13. Pea holder

15. Male adult

16. Highest card

17. They cross avenues: Abbreviation

18. Biblical word of celebration

20. Volleyball game equipment

21. Mined material

22. Golf score

24. Clothes put together as a combination

26. "___, humbug!" (Scrooge's comment)

28. Type of computers: Abbreviation

29. U.S. crime-fighting department: Abbreviation

30. Stuck in a ___ (can't seem to change)

31. Hospital sections that handle accident victims: Abbreviation

32. Sunbeam

33. Little devil

34. Opposite of WNW on a weather vane

35. Distress signal from a sinking ship

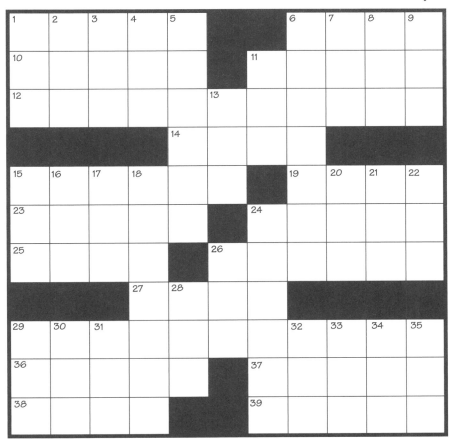

Answers on page 286

# Search for Ss

This picture shows many things that begin with the letter S. Finding at least 30 would be SUPERB. Finding 40 would be SPECTACULAR!

Answers on page 286

# Word Pyramids

Use the clues in parentheses to fill in the missing words in these pyramids. Each level builds on the last one—just add one letter to the previous word, and rearrange the letters as necessary.

1.

        T
__ __ (What "@" means)

__ __ __ (Had dinner)

__ __ __ __ (Place to sit)

__ __ __ __ __ (Captures)

__ __ __ __ __ __ (Person who glides on ice)

__ __ __ __ __ __ __ (Having the least light)

2.

        O
__ __ (Not off)

__ __ __ (Word in the previous clue)

__ __ __ __ (Short message)

__ __ __ __ __ (Small rock)

__ __ __ __ __ __ (Truthful)

__ __ __ __ __ __ __ (Chairs for kings and queens)

__ __ __ __ __ __ __ __ (Opposite of northern)

Answers on page 286

# Frame-Up

Fill the puzzle frame with words that match the clues below. Each word shares one or two letters with the word that comes after it. Start each word in the same space as its clue number. When you get to a corner, follow the direction of the arrow.

Clues

1. Hurry
2. Not tall
3. Journey
4. Very attractive
5. Use the keyboard on a computer
6. Someone who is a nuisance is a _____
7. Melt
8. Horrible!
9. Woman
10. Colored
11. Plate
12. Not a bath

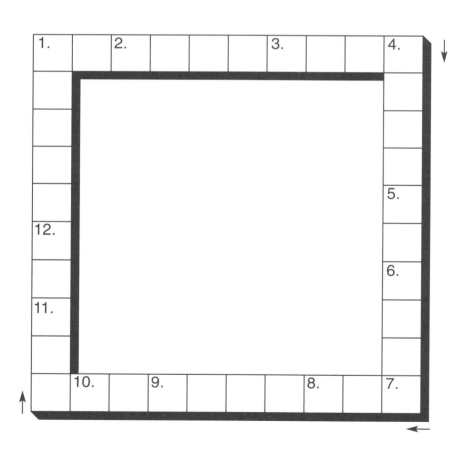

Answers on page 286

# You've Got Mail!

Use the definitions to help you solve this puzzle. Each answer is a word or phrase made up of state postal abbreviations and sometimes additional letters. For example, "Staring at the stars" G/____/____/G would lead to G/AZ/IN/G (gazing). Fill each blank with a two-letter abbreviation from the list below. Some abbreviations will be used two times and are listed twice.

AL AR AR CA CO CO CT DE HI IA ID IN MA MN MO
MS ND NE NH NY OK OK OR PA RI TN

1. They crawl in the soil     W/____/____

2. Does housework     ____/____

3. Take a breath     I/____/____/E

4. Treat for a grown kitten     ____/____/IP

5. Auto trip: 2 words     C/____  ____/____

6. What Santa goes down     C/____/____/EY

7. Recipe guide     ____/____/BO/____

8. Precious jewel     D/____/____/____

9. Your guests     ____/M/____/____

10. Peachlike fruit     ____/____/____/____/E

Answers on page 286

# Crossword

## ACROSS

1. A dunce might have one on his head
4. "Darn it!"
8. Have on
12. State next to Mississippi: Abbreviation
13. Apiece
14. What a saint has above his or her head
15. Sitting on _____ (ecstatic): 4 words
18. Not fresh
19. Ending for "Japan" or "Siam"
20. Father
22. _____ Presley (famous singer)
26. _____ Diego, California
29. 2,000 pounds
31. _____ beam
33. Does something with
35. Sticky stuff
37. What a reporter writes about
38. Scrambled
40. ____ water (what comes out of a faucet)
42. Word ending that means "most"
43. Storage room, sometimes
45. It fits in a lock

47. They aren't yeses
49. Takes a snooze
53. Hole that goes on forever: 2 words
58. Place
59. White stuff on a sandwich, for short
60. "A fool and his money _____ soon parted."
61. Someone between 12 and 20 years old, for short
62. The last word of a hymn
63. _____ York

## DOWN

1. Felines
2. Plenty: 2 words
3. One of the Three Bears
4. Beat in a contest
5. "You dirty _____!"
6. Pain
7. One of _____ days (soon)
8. "Halt! _____ goes there?"
9. You hear with it
10. _____ the time (constantly)
11. Fishing pole
16. Like your great-grandparents
17. Not sick
21. Canine
23. Moving truck

24. "Peekaboo, _____ you!": 2 words
25. Uses a needle and thread
26. Total
27. The largest continent
28. _____-door neighbor
30. "Ready or _____, here I come!"
32. Letters after Q
34. TV _____
36. Kind of tree
39. The Flintstones' pet
41. Individual
44. Punctuation mark that indicates a pause

46. "You bet!"
48. Banging noise
50. Have a short attention _____
51. Spare _____
52. Food that includes meat and potatoes
53. Mammal that hangs upside down
54. It's made into metal
55. A golf ball rests on one
56. Light brown
57. Where the retina and cornea are

Answers on page 286

# Scrambled States

Unscramble the names of these states.

Example:    HOSUT RONAACLI ⟶ SOUTH CAROLINA

1. ATSHAMSCUSETS   __ __ __ __ __ __ (__) __ __ __ __ __

2. NASPLAYENNIV   __ __ (__) __ __ __ __ __ __ __ __

3. IGRANIVI   __ __ __ (__) __ __ __ __

4. CUNETCONCIT   __ __ __ __ __ (__) __ __ __ __ __

5. AGROGIE   __ (__) __ __ __ __ __

6. AMYDRALN   __ __ __ __ __ __ (__) __

7. DREOH DISNAL   __ __ __ __ __ (__) __ __ __ __

8. THORN CLOANRIA   __ __ __ (__) __ __ __ __ __ __ __ __ __ __

9. WEN SPAREHIMH   __ __ __ (__) __ __ __ __ __ __ __

10. ROMVENT   __ __ __ __ __ (__) __

11. ENW KROY   __ (__) __ __ __ __ __

12. WNE SEERJY   __ __ __ __ __ __ (__) __ __

Write the circled letters in order on the lines below to find out a fact about all the states listed above.

They were 12 of the 13 first states to form the

__ __ __ __ __ __ __ __ __ __ __ __ __ __ .

Answers on page 286

# Presidential Nicknames

Did you know that many American presidents had nicknames? Some of them are listed below. Write each president's name beside the matching nickname.

1. Old Rough and Ready _____
   He was given this nickname by his troops who admired his leadership skills in battle.

2. Sage of Monticello _____
   He was named for the many interests he pursued at his home, Monticello.

3. Uncle Jumbo _____
   He was nicknamed for his large size.

4. Peanut Farmer _____
   He was named for the family business he ran.

5. Rough Rider _____
   He was named after the troops that he commanded during the Spanish-American War.

6. Little Ben _____
   He got this nickname from his soldiers because of his small stature.

7. Silent Cal _____
   He was named for his silent, serious nature.

8. The Gipper _____
   He was named for the role he played in the film All American.

9. Old Hickory _____
   He got his name after a soldier remarked that he was as "tough as hickory."

10. Old Man Eloquent _____
    He was named for his superb speaking skills.

Thomas Jefferson
(3rd President)

John Quincy Adams
(6th President)

Andrew Jackson
(7th President)

Zachary Taylor
(12th President)

Grover Cleveland
(22nd and 24th President)

Benjamin Harrison
(23rd President)

Theodore Roosevelt
(26th President)

Calvin Coolidge
(30th President)

Jimmy Carter
(39th President)

Ronald Reagan
(40th President)

Answers on page 286

# Guess the Theme

In this puzzle, the Word list and theme are a secret. It's up to you to figure out what the 20 words in the grid are and what they have in common. In the Word list, you'll find the first letter of each word and the number of letters in it. After you circle an item in the grid, fill in the appropriate blanks in the Word list. If you find a word that doesn't fit in any of the blanks, ignore it: It's not part of the list. In some cases, more than one word will fit a particular set of blanks. Ignore any words that do not have something in common with the other words. Read the uncircled letters from left to right, top to bottom, to reveal the puzzle's theme. We've done one to start you off.

Word list

A C H E

B _ _ _

B _ _ _ _

B _ _ _ _ _ _

D _ _ _ _ _ _

F _ _ _

F _ _ _ _

F _ _ _ _

G _ _ _ _ _

H _ _ _ _

H _ _ _ _

H _ _ _ _

L _ _ _

P _ _ _

P _ _ _ _ _

P _ _ _ _

Q _ _ _ _ _ _ _

S _ _ _ _ _

T _ _ _

Y _ _ _

```
L T A L K C A P A D D
A B B A C K A C T O S
I H T R H P E F H T F
D C O R E O L N R E T
O N R R B A A O Q C D
K U A O S F K E U I B
A H C H F E H E A W O
B Y G G I P O M R R A
D A F O E R O A T N R
E R R W L N W F E E D
O D R E D N U O R G D
```

Theme: _____

_____

Answers on pages 286–287

# Some Dom Questions

Get smart by finding the seven words—all ending in DOM—that answer the following questions. Try it yourself; then try it out on a friend.

1. The DOM that the United States is famous for

_____

2. The DOM that King Solomon and Yoda are famous for

_____

3. The DOM caused by having nothing to do

_____

4. A ruler's DOM

_____

5. The DOM that isn't very often

_____

6. The DOM that is unpredictable

_____

7. The DOM that comes with movie fame

_____

Answers on page 287

# Once Around the Block

Use the clues to fill in the blanks around the block. Start each word in the same space as its clue number. Each word shares one or two letters with the word that comes after it. When you get to a corner, follow the direction of the arrow.

Clues

1. Throw the ball to the catcher in a baseball game
2. Not playing fair
3. Animal who may see his shadow on February 2
4. Shrek is one
5. The planet we live on
6. Use your brain
7. Jousting soldier
8. Flower grown in Holland

Answers on page 287

# Blended Words

A blended word is created by combining parts of two words. Example: *smoke + fog = smog*. Try combining the words below to figure out the blended words.

1. flame + glare = a device that produces a bright light
   __ __ __ __ __

2. squirm + wiggle = a short, wavy line __ __ __ __ __ __ __ __

3. pain + sting = a sudden, sharp ache __ __ __ __

4. motor + hotel = lodging built near a main road __ __ __ __ __

5. sweep + wipe = a sweeping stroke or glancing blow
   __ __ __ __ __

6. blow + spurt = to utter suddenly __ __ __ __ __

7. breakfast + lunch = a meal eaten late in the morning
   __ __ __ __ __ __

8. flap + drop = to fall over loosely __ __ __ __

9. walk + toddle = to walk with short steps, swaying a bit
   __ __ __ __ __ __

10. splash + surge = to spend a lot of money without attention
    to cost __ __ __ __ __ __ __

11. camera + recorder = a device that records sights and sounds
    __ __ __ __ __ __ __ __ __

Answers on page 287

# Eagle Eyes

Here's a riddle: Who can raise things without lifting them? To find the answer, look at every small grid below. One letter of the alphabet has been left out of each grid. Write the missing letter on each line. Then read the letters from 1 to 7 to find the two-word answer.

| F | W | M | V | B |
|---|---|---|---|---|
| J | Q | C | N | G |
| R | D | L | U | X |
| E | P | I | O | Y |
| K | S | T | Z | H |

1. _____

| E | H | P | Q | G |
|---|---|---|---|---|
| S | D | T | W | K |
| U | X | C | J | O |
| Z | V | N | M | B |
| F | Y | I | L | A |

7. _____

| C | M | L | K | J |
|---|---|---|---|---|
| N | B | X | Y | I |
| O | W | A | Z | H |
| P | V | U | D | G |
| Q | R | S | T | F |

6. _____

| E | T | P | V | F |
|---|---|---|---|---|
| X | J | U | W | Y |
| Z | Q | I | R | D |
| C | H | O | N | B |
| G | S | K | L | M |

3. _____

| Z | U | W | C | L |
|---|---|---|---|---|
| Y | V | B | J | K |
| T | A | M | O | D |
| S | X | N | E | I |
| Q | P | F | G | H |

4. _____

| E | L | A | S | F |
|---|---|---|---|---|
| Z | K | G | U | B |
| W | V | H | J | T |
| C | R | I | N | O |
| X | P | Q | Y | D |

5. _____

| Y | G | R | V | W |
|---|---|---|---|---|
| H | X | I | M | D |
| T | N | C | L | Z |
| B | S | K | U | O |
| A | Q | J | P | E |

2. _____

Answer on page 287

249

# Double Wacky Wordies

These words are a wacky way to show a common phrase. In fact, in each example, you'll be seeing double. Study each set of words, and try to solve the riddle.

1.  AROUNDGOING AROUNDGOING  =  _____

2.  SIDE SIDE  =  _____

3.  GNIPMUJ JUMPING  =  _____

4.  PLAY PLAY  =  _____

5.  HOLLYWOOD HOLLYWOOD  =  _____

6.  OVER OVER  =  _____

Answers on page 287

# Amazing Number Pyramid

Write the answer to each problem.
What you'll find is quite amazing!

$0 \times 9 + 1 = $ _____

$1 \times 9 + 2 = $ _____

$12 \times 9 + 3 = $ _____

$123 \times 9 + 4 = $ _____

$1{,}234 \times 9 + 5 = $ _____

$12{,}345 \times 9 + 6 = $ _____

$123{,}456 \times 9 + 7 = $ _____

$1{,}234{,}567 \times 9 + 8 = $ _____

$12{,}345{,}678 \times 9 + 9 = $ _____

**What did you notice about the answers you wrote?**

_____

_____

Answers on page 287

# Crossword

**ACROSS**

1. Sacks
5. Hurt
9. Made-up name
11. _____ energy (energy from the sun)
12. Figures that you move with your fingers: 2 words
14. Take _____ (sleep for a little while): 2 words
15. The cat in *Pinocchio*
19. Pump _____ (lift weights)
23. Love a lot
24. Catch in a trap
25. Part of a house
26. Moved back and forth, like a dog's tail
27. Large tool used by farmers
29. Figures that you move with strings
36. Leaves
37. Serious movie
38. Jewels
39. "Snug as _____ in a rug": 2 words

**DOWN**

1. "_____, humbug!" (what Scrooge said)
2. State next to Georgia: Abbreviation
3. _____ rummy (card game)
4. Unhappy
5. Moving like a rabbit
6. Ginger _____
7. Small rodent
8. Wife's title: Abbreviation
10. _____ change (loose coins)
11. Health resort
13. The Spanish word for "one"
15. Not near
16. "What will _____ now?": 2 words
17. Glop
18. Places to put deodorant
20. Old cloth
21. Metal that's just come out of the ground
22. _____ Flanders (character on *The Simpsons*)
24. Cut with a tool
26. Came in first place

28. _____ Angeles, California
29. Sister in *Little Women*
30. Tool for a lumberjack
31. Edge of a cup
32. "_____ la la" (singing sounds)
33. Pick up the _____ (pay the bill for everyone)
34. Large bird from Australia
35. Droop

| 1 | 2 | 3 | 4 | ■ | ■ | ■ | 5 | 6 | 7 | 8 |
|---|---|---|---|---|---|---|---|---|---|---|
| 9 | | | | 10 | ■ | 11 | | | | |
| 12 | | | | | 13 | | | | | |
| ■ | ■ | ■ | ■ | 14 | | | | ■ | ■ | ■ |
| 15 | 16 | 17 | 18 | | | ■ | 19 | 20 | 21 | 22 |
| 23 | | | | | ■ | 24 | | | | |
| 25 | | | | ■ | 26 | | | | | |
| ■ | ■ | ■ | 27 | 28 | | | ■ | ■ | ■ | ■ |
| 29 | 30 | 31 | | | | | 32 | 33 | 34 | 35 |
| 36 | | | | | ■ | 37 | | | | |
| 38 | | | | ■ | ■ | ■ | 39 | | | |

Answers on page 287

# Something's Missing

This puzzle is like a normal word search—except one letter in each word is missing in the grid. (For example, ANTIDOTE might be in the grid as NTIDOTE or ATIDOTE.) Write the missing letters from the top to the bottom of the Word list to get an appropriate message.

Word list

Antidote
Basketball
Breastbone
Cooperative
Dumplings
Education
Exhaling
Filmstrip
Gateway
Hijinks
Hillier
Ickiest
Letters
Mammoth
Melted
Naughty
Needier
Optional
Rubbing
Safety
Sign up
Strands
Thousand
Tweezers

Unfortunately
Violinist
Watermelon
Windmill
Xylophone
Yesterday

```
V V H M O X B Y T G U A N
I R I L L I H M A M M O T
L R J T L D N A S U H T I
I P I E A S G I L P M U D
N I N D T R L N O I T P O
I R S R E T E L I S N L T
S T S A K E Y P I B E G E
T S R S S X N N O M B C G
Y L E T A N U T R O N U T
E I Z A B P T E I K C I E
F F E N O B T A E R B M W
A P E D U A T I O N Q N A
S L T S W Y E S T E D A Y
```

Message: _____

_____

_____

_____

Answers on page 287

# What's Wrong in Time?

Take a look at this picture, and you'll see what it was like to be a kid living during the colonial days of George Washington. Everything here looks just like it did more than 200 years ago. But wait...how did that get in there? It seems our artist made a mistake, accidentally adding a few things that weren't yet invented in 1776. Find ten out-of-time objects.

Answers on page 287

# Computer Know-How

Use the definitions and picture clues to find each computer term. Then write the circled letters on the numbered lines to answer the riddle.

1. start your computer  __ __ ◯ __

2. computer shut down  ◯ __ __ __ __

3. open or start a program  __ __ __ __ __ ◯

4. list of screen commands  ◯ __ __ __

5. handheld device that clicks  __ __ __ ◯ __

6. machine that puts text on paper  __ __ ◯ __ __ __ __

7. to copy and place text  ◯ __ __ __ __

8. program that harms a computer  __ ◯ __ __

9. abbreviation that stands for "random access memory"  ◯ __ __

10. it reads your photos and documents  __ ◯ __ __ __ __

Riddle: What is a computer's favorite snack food?

Answer: __ __ __ __ __ __ __ __ __ __ __ !
    4  6  10  9  1  2  3  8  7  5

Answers on page 287

# Sixes and Sevens

Join together two letter groups from the box below to make a 6- or 7-letter word that answers each clue. Write each word into the grid, going down. Be sure to match the number in the grid with the clue number. Cross off each letter group as you use it. When the grid is filled, read the circled letters from left to right to find the answer to this joke: Why didn't the seafood salad get along with the rest of the meal?

## Clues

1. Not public
2. Very smart
3. Speak in a very low voice
4. Breathe out
5. You drink beverages from these
6. "Lights, camera, ____ !"
7. The coldest part of a refrigerator
8. Duck sounds
9. Bed cover
10. Log homes
11. Major road for traveling

| ACT | ALE | BLAN | BRI | CAB |
| CKS | EXH | FREE | GHT | GLAS |
| HIGH | INS | ION | KET | PER |
| PRI | QUA | SES | VATE | WAY |
| | WHIS | ZER | | |

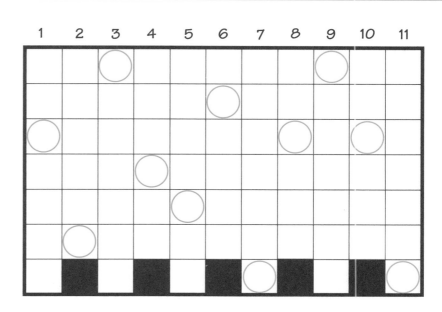

Answer: _____

Answers on page 287

# Once Around the Big Block

Use the clues to fill in the blanks around the block. Start each word in the same space as its clue number. Each word will start with the last two letters of the word that comes right before it. When you get to a corner, follow the direction of the arrow.

## Clues

1. Tank in which to keep fish
2. **Person who calls balls and strikes**
3. One of the two major political parties in the United States.
4. **Joint near your foot**
5. Drink you might sell at a stand
6. **Person who cleans your teeth**
7. Ohio or Texas, for example
8. **Awful**
9. Strap for holding onto a dog
10. **Short version of the name of a really big pro basketball star**

Answers on page 288

# Palindrome Search

A *palindrome* is a word or phrase that reads the same
both forward and backward. For example,
*dud* and *don't nod* are palindromes. Circle the 26
palindromes in the puzzle below.
The words go across, down, and diagonally.

```
O  O  T  H  A  E  R  I  P  P  I  N  N  U  N
M  A  O  R  E  P  A  P  E  R  T  D  I  B  A
A  O  O  D  K  R  C  T  I  V  R  A  D  A  R
I  T  M  R  A  O  E  N  J  Z  O  D  O  T  A
N  O  A  A  T  O  C  E  W  E  N  P  A  D  S
O  O  R  W  A  S  A  Y  O  O  U  R  S  R  C
O  I  O  N  P  Z  R  N  D  P  K  A  Y  A  K
N  D  A  I  O  A  G  O  R  R  I  T  S  L  T
H  I  R  N  P  S  D  N  O  T  A  T  O  N  O
O  D  S  W  O  E  O  G  A  G  M  O  L  T  O
E  D  E  A  R  E  L  D  E  E  D  O  O  S  T
B  I  B  R  O  S  T  I  L  L  A  R  S  B  P
R  A  R  D  T  O  T  K  E  Y  E  E  R  E  S
C  I  V  I  C  O  O  I  A  G  E  N  E  G  E
O  O  N  E  L  E  V  E  L  B  L  P  O  N  E
```

Answers on page 288

# Three in a Row

Fill in the blanks with three consecutive letters to make words. Consecutive letters follow one after the other, like A, B, and C or D, E, and F.

1. F I __ __ __

2. L A U __ __ __ N G

3. __ __ __ E A T

4. __ __ __ D Y

5. __ __ __ A C K

6. U __ __ __ E N E D

7. A __ __ __ A N

8. W O __ __ __

Now fill in the blanks with three consecutive letters that are in backward order, such as C, B, and A or F, E, and D.

9. __ __ __ Y

10. G O L __ __ __

11. P E A N __ __ __

12. R E S __ __ __ D

Answers on page 288

# Mixed Messages

Here are three riddles:

1. What bow can never be tied?

2. What do you call a fast tricycle?

3. What has fingers and thumbs but no arms?

The answers to these riddles are hidden in the box below. To find the answer for Riddle 1, copy all the letters above the numeral 1. Go in order from left to right and then top to bottom, and put each letter into a blank space below. Do the same thing for the numerals 2 and 3 to get the answers for Riddles 2 and 3.

| A | A | G | T | R | L | O |
|---|---|---|---|---|---|---|
| 1 | 2 | 3 | 2 | 1 | 3 | 2 |
| O | A | T | V | R | I | N |
| 3 | 1 | 2 | 3 | 2 | 1 | 1 |
| B | E | O | O | S | W | D |
| 1 | 3 | 1 | 2 | 3 | 1 | 2 |

Answer to Riddle 1: __ __ __ __ __ __ __ __ __ __

Answer to Riddle 2: __ __ __ __ __ __ __ __

Answer to Riddle 3: __ __ __ __ __ __ __

Answers on page 288

# Crossword

1. Not shut
5. Toy that spins
8. Moves a boat
12. Encourage
13. Female sheep
14. Garfield's friend
15. Kind of drink: 2 words
17. _____ Lisa (famous painting)
18. Go off the deep _____ (go crazy)
19. There are 52 of them in a deck
20. Lift up
24. Religious woman
25. Measure of land
26. "X marks the _____"
28. Fuel for an automobile
31. Kind of drink: 2 words
34. Ex-boyfriend of Barbie
35. What Tarzan swings on
36. "So what _____ is new?"
37. Jewel
38. Permit
39. Kind of drink
42. What a happy dog's tail does
44. "Peekaboo, _____ you!": 2 words
45. Kind of drink
50. The Seven Deadly _____

51. "Just who do you think you _____?"
52. Bad sign for the future
53. Despise
54. Ballpoint _____
55. Begin to droop, like a sick flower

1. Your and my
2. Athlete who gets paid
3. What a vain person has a lot of
4. You can catch fish in it
5. Someone who's not 20 yet
6. Needed to pay back
7. Miles _____ hour
8. From the capital of Italy
9. Smell
10. Breeze
11. Sail the seven _____
16. Insect that loves flowers
19. Adorable
20. You might hang a coat on one
21. Sore spot
22. It gets the wrinkles out of clothes
23. Part of a minute: Abbreviation
24. Short letter
26. Thin
27. Peter _____

28. Something a fish breathes with

29. Not to mention

30. Move on a slant

32. Opposite of under

33. _____ Blanc (the voice of Bugs Bunny)

37. Birds that fly in a V formation

38. Long _____ (in the distant past)

39. Desire

40. Continent next to Europe

41. What a camper sleeps in

42. "Those _____ the days"

43. Word at the end of a prayer

45. You might put your napkin on it

46. At this very moment

47. "What _____ supposed to do?": 2 words

48. The first state in the U.S.: Abbreviation

49. Ending for the word "differ"

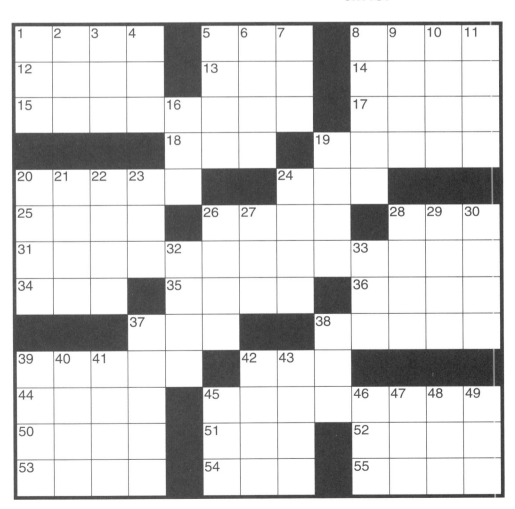

Answers on page 288

# You've Got Mail!

Use the definitions to help you solve this puzzle. Each answer is a word or phrase made up of state postal abbreviations and sometimes additional letters. For example, "Staring at the stars" G/____/____/G would lead to G/AZ/IN/G (gazing). Fill in each blank with a two-letter abbreviation from the list below. Some abbreviations will be used two different times and are listed twice.

AK AL AL AZ CA CA CO CO DE DE FL GA HI IL KS
LA ME MI NC ND NE OR PA RI SC SD UT VA WI

1. Red Sox event: 2 words B/____/L ____/____

2. Squeezes a dairy cow M/____/____

3. Shaving tool R/____/____

4. Snow particle ____/____/E

5. Outlaw's secret place ____/____/O/____

6. Write or tell about ____/____/____/BE

7. Pepsi rival ____/____ - ____/____

8. Goof up handing out cards ____/____/E/____

9. Sign at a full motel: 2 words NO ____/____/____/Y

10. Part of a wall opening ____/____/OW/____/____

Answers on page 288

# Number Patterns

Look at the rows of numbers. Each row has its own pattern. Figure out the patterns, and then add three more numbers to each row.

1. 12, 23, 34, 45, _____, _____, _____

2. 0, 1, 3, 6, 10, 15, _____, _____, _____

3. 19, 28, 37, 46, 55, _____, _____, _____

4. 0, 5, 4, 9, 8, 13, 12, _____, _____, _____

5. 1, 1, 2, 4, 3, 9, 4, 16, _____, _____, _____

6. 0, 1, 1, 2, 3, 5, 8, 13, _____, _____, _____

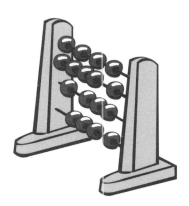

Look at the numbers in each box. Tell how they are alike.

7.
| 36 | 48 |
| 84 | 24 | 12 |
| 21 | 63 |

_____

_____

8.
| 242 | 396 |
| 187 | 352 |
| 561 | 264 |

_____

_____

9.
| 321 | 432 |
| 975 | 789 | 456 |
| 543 | 999 |

_____

_____

Answers on page 288

# Finish Lines

Every book has to come to an end, so our final word search contains words and phrases said before leaving or ending. Because the puzzles are coming to a stop, the grid is in the shape of a stop sign. As usual, words in the grid will go across, backward, up, down, and diagonally but always in a straight line. Circle the words as you find them in the grid, and cross them off the list. When you're done, read the uncircled letters in the grid from left to right, top to bottom, to spell out three more phrases that are famous last words.

**Word list**

Adios
Aloha
Bye now
Call it a day
Ciao
Finish
Halt
Hasta la vista
Later
No more
Party's over
Quit
See ya
So long
Stop
Ta-ta
That's all, folks
Time to go

```
            T H H A Q
          C I A O U Y A
        T Y S S I A W E R
      A P A R T Y S O V E R
    L T P D H A D I O S O S P
    A E A A Y L H S I N I F O
    T H A T S A L L F O L K S
    E U O I A V H A D M S F W
    R T U L T I M E T O G O N
      S L L A S E E L R N Y
      O A U T T O A E G
        C H A N O Y A
          I G N B P
```

Answers: _____

Answers on page 288

# ANSWERS

## What's at the Theater? (page 4)

1. movie; 2. popcorn; 3. soda;
4. tickets; 5. candy

## Out of Place (page 5)

1. plane; 2. watch; 3. cat;
4. book; 5. house; 6. family

## True or False (page 6)

Neptune

## Bee Quick (page 7)

## For the Birds (page 8)

## A Matter of Taste (page 9)

The word is CHIP.

## Ann E. Gram (page 10)

nest = sent, shoe = hose, ends
= dens, lose = sole, part =
trap, bowl = blow, life = file

## High Flying (page 11)

## Wild Cats (page 12)

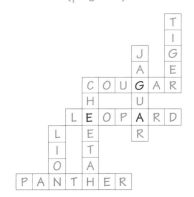

## "E" Words (page 13)

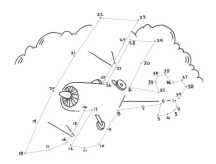

## Step by Step (page 14)

## Cross It Out (page 15)

Your age

## Fruit Salad (page 16)

## Lost Planet Maze (page 17)

267

## What's Your Number? (page 18)

## Works of Art (page 19)

1. tray; 2. star; 3. train; 4. heart; 5. earth; 6. feather; 7. triangle

## Tiny Creatures (page 20)

1. ant; 2. bee; 3. fly; 4. moth; 5. snail; 6. wasp

## Gigantic Creatures (page 20)

1. python; 2. crocodile; 3. hippopotamus; 4. rhinoceros; 5. giraffe; 6. elephant

## Picture Crossword (page 21)

## It's a Hot One Today (page 22)

## Bible Fun (page 23)

1. Please bring a bell to school. 2. They went to the spa ultimately. 3. The car got stuck in a rut here in town. 4. Seven can play this game at home. 5. The ape terrified the children. 6. Britney owned the only diary. 7. On your nose is a mosquito. 8. Ma, rye bread or white bread? 9. There should be no cracks in a dam. 10. My cat teases the rabbit at night.

## Word Play (page 24)

multiply, above, rough, young, loosen, absent, narrow, difficult;

**Riddle answer:** Maryland (merry land)

## Getting There (page 25)

## A Classroom Puzzle (page 26)

1. clock; 2. flag; 3. paper; 4. desk; 5. stapler; 6. ruler; 7. book; 8. globe; 9. marker

## Ant Words (page 27)

pants, plant, against, planet, antique

## Ruff! (page 27)

dough, dodge, drought, undoing, headlong

## Letters in Colors (page 28)

green, yellow

## Add a Letter (page 29)

Add a T to spell told, tear, tart, that, till, trim, this, tail, tore, task.

## Step by Step (page 30)

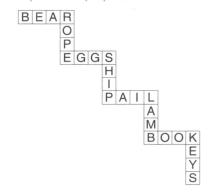

## Jurassic Jerry (page 31)

## G Is for Guessing (page 32)

game, garbage can, garden, gardener, gas can, gate, ghost, giant, giraffe, girl, glasses, glider, globe, gloves, goal, goalie, goat, goggles, goose, gorilla, grades, grapes, grass, grate, grill, guard, gum (other answers are possible)

## A Shirt Riddle (page 33)

Your belly button

## Name Game (page 34)

## Vowels in the City (page 35)

1. New York; 2. Los Angeles;
3. Chicago; 4. Houston;
5. Philadelphia; 6. Phoenix;
7. San Diego; 8. San Antonio;
9. Dallas; 10. Detroit

## A Trail of Threes (page 36)

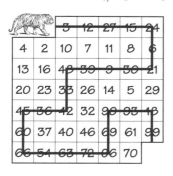

## State Lines (page 37)

Louisiana

## Hidden Numbers (page 38)

1. two; 2. seven; 3. five;
4. six; 5. ten; 6. eight; 7. nine;
8. three; 9. one; 10. four

## Parachute Words (page 39)

```
C H A P T E R        P
R          E     R    A
A          A     A    R
T          C A R P E T
E A R T H             
     C        H E A R T
P U T         A       E
     T        R       A
T E A C U P   CAR
```

## Mystery Words (page 40)

1. eagle; 2. maple; 3. collie;
4. plum; 5. trout; 6. golf

## Change to Sport (page 41)

1. soccer; 2. baseball;
3. football; 4. tennis;
5. golf; 6. basketball.

## Puzzling Animals (page 41)

ant, pony, robin, beaver, mouse, porcupine

## Good Dog (page 42)

## Up Front (page 43)

middle, omelet, octopus, silly, icing, cave, almost, little, carrot, happy, ambulance, igloo, roar, stand
Riddle answer: Moosical chairs (musical chairs)

## Special Day (page 44)

```
A S H E S
  B A R K
C A L L
D E A L
E N J O Y
F L O W E R
    G E E S E
H O M E
    I N K
```

Halloween

## Letter Moving (page 45)

Little Jack Horner sat in a corner.

## Volcano Maze (page 46)

### Colorful Puddles (page 47)

1. blue; 2. red; 3. green;
4. yellow; 5. brown; 6. white;
7. black; 8. pink; 9. gray

### Desserts Crisscross (page 48)

### Car Fun (page 49)

1. cart; 2. card; 3. scarf;
4. carry; 5. scare;
6. carve; 7. carrot;
8. cartoon; 9. carp;
10. carpet; 11. carton;
12. carpenter

### Ooooh! (page 50)

### A Special Gift (page 51)

1. s; 2. a; 3. i; 4. l; 5. b; 6. o;
7. a; 8. t
(A sailboat should be drawn
in the box.)

### Look a Round (page 52)

1. I saw he elbowed his way
through the crowd. 2. Today's
good, but tonight isn't.
3. "Online I use Yahoo," Peter
said. 4. Dancers like soft
ballet slippers. 5. I have
to wash a load of laundry.
6. Who was your teacher
in grade school? 7. In Iowa
I stood in a cornfield.
8. Where's the bag Elmo
brought? 9. Why can't I re ad
your letter out loud?

### People Crisscross (page 53)

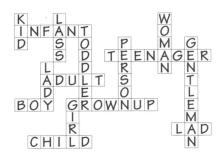

### Website (page 54)

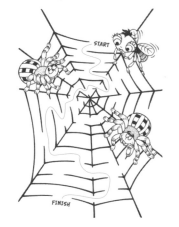

### C-Ya (page 55)

1. face; 2. sun; 3. corn;
4. book; 5. church;
6. clock; 7. chicken

### Look for These Cs (page 56)

cactus, calendar, camel,
candles, candy, car, carrot,
castle, cat, caterpillar, cheese,
cherry, chicks, chip, chocolate,
circle, city, clock, cloud, coin,
cookie, corn, cow, cowboy,
crayon

### Flight Plan (page 57)

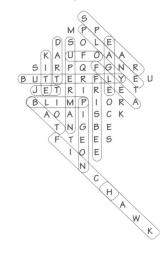

### Paint a Picture (page 58)

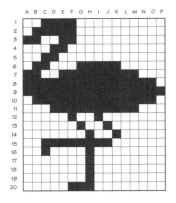

flamingo

## Blended Crisscrosses (page 59)

```
B E E           T
E       F L E A  E
D       L     M  R
B       Y     O  M
U             T  I
G N A T          T
        H O R N E T
```

```
        S
    B R O O M
    U       O
    C   S   P
    K       B
    E       L
    T O W E L
            A
            C
    B R U S H
```

## Animal Maker (page 60)

1. cat; 2. dog; 3. goat; 4. pig;
5. duck; 6. bat; 7. snake;
8. shark; 9. crab/grub; 10. fox;
11. bear; 12. ant; 13. seal;
14. bee; 15. whale; 16. clam;
17. deer; 18. fly; 19. owl;
20. parrot; 21. eel; 22. frog;
23. beaver; 24. sloth;
25. swan; 26. toad; 27. worm;
28. stork

## Stargazing (page 61)

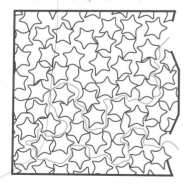

## ABC Code (page 62)

1. What kind of birthday did
the frog have? A hoppy one.

2. Why does a dog wag its
tail? Because no one will wag
it for him. 3. What do you
call a cow eating grass?
**Answer:** a lawn moo-er.

## Another True or False (page 63)

spinach

## Too Much (page 64)

Parts of the Body: arms,
fingers; Farm Animals: horse,
pig; Vegetables: peas, corn;
Meats: steak, bacon; Birds:
crow, eagle; Numbers: thirty,
eighty; Bodies of Water: lake,
pond; Musical Instruments:
horn, harp; Planets: Earth,
Mars; Desserts: ice cream,
apple pie

## Sun Fun (page 65)

1. sunrise; 2. sunset;
3. sunglasses; 4. sunscreen;
5. sunshine; 6. sundial;
7. sunflower; 8. suntan;
9. sunbeam; 10. sunburn

## Mystery Star (page 66)

```
        B A B Y
    C H U R C H
            S I N G E R
F O U N D A T I O N
    M A D O N N A
        K E N T W O O D
        Y O U N G
    M O U S E
O V E R P R O T E C T E D
    D E C E M B E R
    A W A R D S
    C U R I O U S
C R O S S R O A D S
```

Britney Spears

## Clothes Lines (page 67)

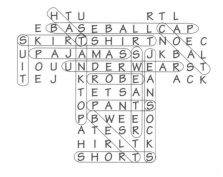

## Haunted House Maze (page 68)

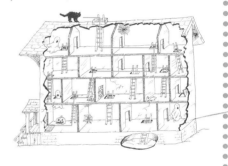

## Triplets (page 69)

carpets, mushrooms

## Going in Circles (page 70)

clock, top, watch, wheel,
planet, track, carousel, electron

## Mix and Match (page 71)

1. pancake; 2. inkstand;
3. online; 4. potbelly;
5. damage; 1. teammate;
2. target; 3. pitfall; 4. dewdrop;
5. gummy; 1. itself; 2. making;
3. teardrop; 4. slapstick;
5. barefoot

## Dollars and Cents (page 72)

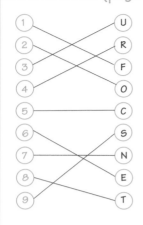

four cents

## In D (page 73)

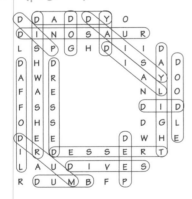

## Add a Word (page 74)

1. forget, fortune, forgive, forbid; 2. cargo, carton, carpet, carrot; 3. manor, manage, manhunt, mandate

## An Apple a Day (page 75)

## Picture Crossword (page 76)

## Crack the Code (page 77)

One hundred sows and bucks!

## 'Tis the Season (page 78)

1. winter; 2. puddle; 3. snow; 4. lightning; 5. fog; 6. storm; 7. summer; 8. wind; 9. thunder; 10. autumn; **Answer to riddle:** Springtime!

## Time and Hair (page 79)

Time: tame, tile, tiny, lime, tree
Hair: fair, hard, hail, pair, half

## Paint a Picture (page 80)

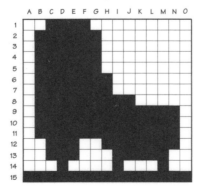

ice skate

## Water Wonders (page 81)

It was nice running into you.

## Trivial Quiz (page 82)

1. bowling ball; 2. Tuesday; 3. popcorn; 4. sheep; 5. right elbow; 6. Clinton

## In Outer Space (page 83)

1. sun; 2. planet; 3. star; 4. comet; 5. meteor; 6. spacecraft; 7. orbit; 8. moon

## Mystery Musician (page 84)

Stevie Wonder

## Doubles (page 85)

The extra word is "hero." The meanings of this word are "a brave person" and "a large sandwich."

## Place Mats (page 86)

1. Baltimore & Oregon
2. Milan & Lancaster
3. Louisiana & Anaheim
4. Princeton & Tonga
5. Turkey & Key West
6. Florida & Idaho
7. Newark & Arkansas
8. Cleveland & Andover
9. Dresden & Denver
10. Amsterdam & Damascus

11. Oslo & Slovakia
12. Japan & Panama
13. Augusta & Stamford
14. Hoboken & Kentucky

### What's in Common? (page 87)

If you move the S from the end of each word to its front, you get a new word: snail, swing, smile, strap, scold, space, stale, sweep, shoot, and spear.

### Word Families (page 88)

1. also, half, whale, animal; 2. stop, touch, cotton, potato; 3. pick, pupil, copier, jumping; 4. zero, gaze, buzzer, sneezed

### Jordan's Story (page 89)

1. York; 2. store; 3. for; 4. boring; 5. sore; 6. corner; 7. ignoring; 8. sorry; 9. forgive; 10. forty; 11. shorts; 12. more

### School Daze (page 90)

1. geography; 2. history; 3. reading; 4. spelling; 5. arithmetic; 6. teacher; 7. principal; 8. library; 9. student; 10. grammar; 11. literature; 12. homework

### Tricky Tongue Twisters (page 91)

1. Seven snakes slithered silently; 2. Busy bakers busily baked bread; 3. Peggy painted pretty purple parrots; 4. Winnie waited while Warren went walking; 5. Grant grows green grass; 6. Lily likes licking lollipops; 7. Troy's train tooted two times; 8. Rob rows rowboats rapidly; 9. Ned's nine newts nibbled nuts; 10. Four fireflies flew from France.

### Outer Space Word Search (page 92)

| A | S | T | R | O | N | A | U | T | P | R | O |
| N | O | O | M | M | N | U | S | T | O | M | E |
| M | E | T | E | O | R | I | T | E | T | E | A |
| O | L | S | U | V | W | I | L | N | U | R | R |
| S | G | R | E | I | C | L | A | A | L | C | T |
| G | R | B | E | R | A | M | S | L | P | U | H |
| D | R | B | E | A | T | T | P | D | R | R | E |
| R | S | A | I | T | S | A | Q | A | M | Y | W |
| O | O | S | U | M | S | R | P | L | G | I | K |
| B | I | G | D | I | P | P | E | R | L | Y | S |

### Up Front (page 93)

1. web; 2. bus; 3. name; 4. head; 5. cherry; 6. chimney; 7. dishes; 8. with; 9. anthem; 10. heather/weather; 11. melt; 12. kite; 13. use/wee; 14. shell/swell; 15. whimper/whisper; 16. awe; 17. thimble; 18. chest; 19. teacher; 20. history; 21. jewel; 22. camel; 23. youth; 24. little; 25. help; 26. crust; 27. young; 28. chime; 29. washer; 30. whisker

### Eliminations (page 94)

on an eye land ("island")

### Scrambled Sports (page 95)

1. in, nest, tennis; 2. fall, boot, football; 3. is, king, skiing; 4. lab, bales, baseball; 5. blast, bleak, basketball

### Find the Football (page 96)

1. Do I get a quarter back in change from my dollar? 2. It was the first downpour of the rainy season. 3. Tampa's stadium gets very full on Sundays. 4. The secretary had to stack letters for her boss. 5. Ethel met Lucy at the TV studio. 6. The spider spun terrible webs. 7. The angry boy pulled the second hand off of the watch. 8. Finding the computer room open, Al typed up the list. 9. Is that clover Tim eats for a snack? 10. Sue's house is as big a mess as you'll ever see.

### Hidden Animals (page 97)

1. dog; 2. eel; 3. bat; 4. monkey; 5. pig; 6. cat; 7. toad; 8. lion; 9. eagle; 10. deer; 11. fly
**Answer to riddle:** They use camel-flage!

### Anthill (page 98)

## What a Year! (page 99)

month, week, second, calendar, minute, day, hour, season, year; twenty-one

## Famous Tales and Rhymes (page 100)

1. Humpty Dumpty
2. Simple Simon
3. Georgie Porgie
4. Sleeping Beauty
5. Ugly Duckling
6. Little Mermaid

## Around the House (page 101)

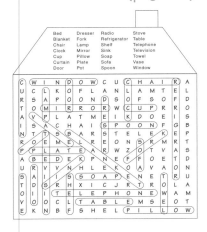

## Word Magic (page 102)

1. cat, rat, rag, rug; 2. leg, log, dog, doe; 3. sun, bun, bud, bed

## Bowling Blunders (page 103)

boy on skateboard, missing lane 4, turtle as bowling ball, soldier as pin, hoop on lane, three bowling balls on one lane, girl bowling wrong way, upside down bowling pin, skeeball target in place of pins, barefoot boy, oversize shoe, duck and water in alley, upside down glasses, beachball, "Pineheads"

## Pinball Panic (page 104)

## "C" First Americans (page 105)

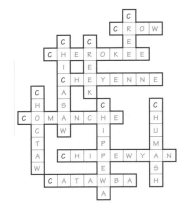

## Eliminations (page 106)

Why are farmers so smart?

## Recipe for Fun (page 107)

He felt crummy.

## Paint a Picture (page 108)

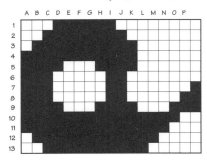

tape dispenser

## It's in the Cards (page 109)

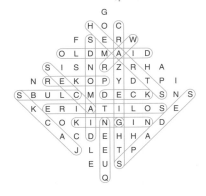

## Famous Cities and Countries (page 110)

1. Paris, France
2. Toronto, Canada
3. Moscow, Russia
4. Beijing, China
5. Cancun, Mexico
6. Jerusalem, Israel

## Where's the Wood? (page 111)

1. Where was he going? 2. Here's the violin Dennis bought. 3. I can make it if I rush. 4. I'm a pleasant person. 5. Let's go to a kite store. 6. She didn't like the bony fish. 7. The store president said, "Hello customers." 8. They wanted to live in Alaska. 9. This is the cap I need. 10. We'll play outside when the haze lifts. 11. The principal made a speech. 12. She placed a rose on the chair.

## F Is for Finding (page 112)

faces, fairy, false teeth, fan, farm, farmer, feather, feet, fence, Ferris wheel, fin, fingers, fire, firefighters, fire truck, fireworks, fish, fist, flag, flames, flash (on camera), flashlight, flat tire, float, flowers, flute, fly, food, football, footstool, forest, fort, fountain, fox, frame, freezer, French horn, fridge, frog, fruit, fur coat (other answers are possible)

## End of the Line (page 113)

Quebec, pencil, nightmare, fever, stick, shark, judge, marathon, quartet

**Answer:** Clerk Kent

## Shh! (page 114)

## Scrambled Opposites (page 115)

1. front and back; 2. high and low; 3. kind and cruel; 4. laugh and cry; 5. lose and find; 6. loud and soft; 7. neat and messy; 8. never and always; 9. raise and lower; 10. rich and poor; 11. save and spend; 12. start and finish; 13. true and false; 14. weak and strong; 15. wild and tame

## Shared Words (page 116)

1. guitar & target
2. parrot & rotten
3. alphabet & better
4. napkin & kindness
5. pelican & candle
6. opera & eraser
7. sudden & dentist
8. luggage & agent
9. brother & hermit
10. repair & airport
11. infant & antelope
12. depart & article

## Alphabet Soup (page 117)

1. school; 2. favors; 3. tomato; 4. liquid; 5. canary; 6. wicked; 7. yogurt; 8. hijack; 9. inform; 10. carton; 11. student; 12. Mexico; 13. flying; 14. habits; 15. graded; 16. rescue; 17. dozens; 18. profit; 19. vowels; 20. triple; 21. bakery; 22. steady; 23. expect; 24. calmer; 25. future; 26. judges

## Trivia Quiz (page 118)

1. spider; 2. Washington, D.C.; 3. radio; 4. tennis player; 5. triangle; 6. eye

## Missing Link (page 119)

## Trees Crisscross (page 120)

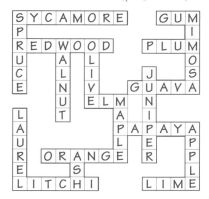

## The IN Crowd (page 121)

1. INk; 2. INch; 3. INdex; 4. INjury; 5. INdoors; 6. INternet; 7. INvisible; 8. INcomplete; 9. INformation; 10. INdependence

## Country Balloons (page 122)

1. Peru; 2. Kenya; 3. India; 4. Japan; 5. Egypt; 6. Spain; 7. Korea; 8. Brazil; 9. England
**Answer:** Australia

## Find the Missing Letters (page 123)

1. boat, belt, Bart; 2. cart, coat, colt; 3. dart, dent, dirt; 4. fast, fist, fort; 5. must, meet, moat

## One Word, Different Meanings (page 124)

1. tires; 2. bear; 3. can; 4. light; 5. line; 6. pack

## What Am I? (page 125)

a joke

## A Learning Experience (page 126)

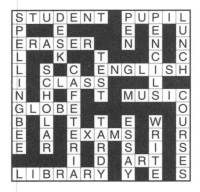

## Mix and Match Again (page 127)

1. racetrack, 2. ringleader, 3. skateboard, 4. stopwatch, 5. eastbound; 1. steamboat, 2. scarlet, 3. lifetime, 4. doorknob, 5. breakfast; 1. spaceship, 2. trapdoor, 3. limelight, 4. broadcast, 5. threesome

## Add-ons (page 128)

1. below; 2. handsome; 3. popcorn; 4. robin; 5. solid; 6. carton; 7. today; 8. logjam; 9. password; 10. package; 11. attire; 12. donkey; 13. hogwash; 14. bandage

## At the Plate (page 129)

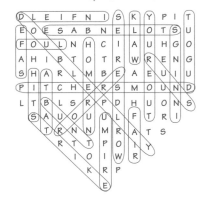

pinch hitter, ball, shortstop

## Number Challenge (page 130)

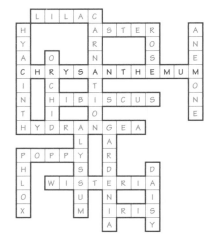

## Surroundings (page 131)

1. copycat; 2. contest; 3. package; 4. poorest; 5. tadpole; 6. shallow; 7. miracle; 8. recital; 9. machine; 10. publish; 11. shampoo; 12. pasture; 13. nearest; 14. daycare

## A Word Train (page 132)

1. zebra; 2. rainbow; 3. owed; 4. edge; 5. general; 6. almost; 7. station; 8. once; 9. center; 10. erase; 11. seesaw; 12. awesome; 13. mean; 14. anchor; 15. order

## Flowers Galore! (page 133)

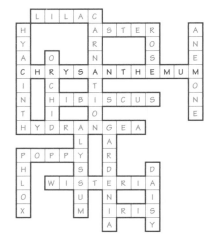

## Tourist Attractions (page 134)

1. Betsy Ross House
2. Alcatraz Island
3. Empire State Building
4. Epcot Center
5. Franklin Institute
6. Getty Museum
7. Golden Gate Bridge
8. Liberty Bell
9. Sears Tower
10. Space Needle
11. Statue of Liberty
12. White House

## Crossword (page 135)

## More Scrambled Sports (page 136)

1. fur, sing, surfing; 2. ball, lovely, volleyball; 3. ark, tea, karate; 4. glow, bin, bowling; 5. grin, nun, running

## Word Magic (page 137)

1. saw, paw, pan, pen
2. pin, pie, tie, toe
3. cap, cup, cub, tub

## Mystery Letters (page 138)

1. colors of a rainbow—red, orange, yellow, green, blue, indigo, violet
2. seasons—winter, spring, summer, fall
3. planets—Mercury, Venus, Earth, Mars, Jupiter, Saturn, Uranus, Neptune, Pluto
4. days of the week—Monday, Tuesday, Wednesday, Thursday, Friday, Saturday, Sunday
5. numbers—one, two, three, four, five
6. oceans—Pacific, Atlantic, Arctic, Indian

7. Great Lakes—Huron, Ontario, Michigan, Erie, Superior

## Desert Crossing (page 139)

a thirst aid kit

## Word Maze (page 140)

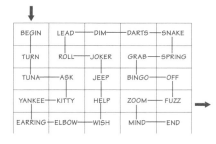

## Grand Opening (page 141)

1. burp; 2. listen;
3. telephone; 4. holiday;
5. quiz; 6. grandfather;
7. people; 8. volleyball;
9. dragon; 10. silver;
11. order; 12. which;
13. apple; 14. juice;
15. neighbor; 16. flagpole;
17. easy; 18. zebra;
19. xylophone; 20. icicle;
21. reindeer; 22. usually;
23. mistletoe; 24. yogurt;
25. crazy; 26. kangaroo

## City's Silly Phrases (page 142)

1. l; 2. j; 3. h; 4. g; 5. k; 6. i;
7. b; 8. e; 9. a; 10. c; 11. d; 12. f

## Mixed Messages (page 143)

1. your picture
2. a hot dog
3. to the lunch counter

## Silly Rhymes (page 144)

1. Delaware (small state)
2. Reese Witherspoon (actress who starred in *Legally Blonde* and *Just Like Heaven*)
3. Babe Ruth (one of the greatest baseball players of all times)
4. *Freaky Friday* (movie about a mother and daughter switching places)
5. Peter Pan (fictional boy who refuses to grow up)
6. Backstreet Boys (boy band with the hit song "Incomplete")
7. Bow Wow (rapper whose name sounds like a dog's bark)
8. New York Knicks (basketball team)
9. Lance Armstrong (cyclist who won the Tour de France seven times)
10. Bill Gates (very rich founder of Microsoft)
11. Saint Paul (capital of Minnesota)
12. Super Bowl (major football event)

## Start/Finish (page 145)

sunscream

## Word Pyramids (page 146)

1. a; 2. an; 3. ran; 4. rain;
5. train; 6. strain; 1. i; 2. it;
3. pit; 4. spit; 5. spite; 6. sprite

## Fivers (page 147)

Birds: 1. raven; 2. goose;
3. robin; 4. stork; 5. eagle
Foreign countries: 1. India;
2. Japan; 3. Egypt; 4. China;
5. Spain

## Magic Word Squares (page 148)

### Square #1

### Square #2

### Square #3

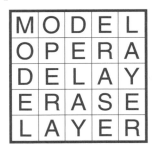

## What's Going On? (page 149)

(The digits are added each time until a number between 1 and 9 is reached.)
1. 43; 7 2. 18; 9 3. 60; 6 4. 78; 15; 6 5. 94; 13; 4 6. 416; 11; 2 7. 2,577; 21; 3 8. 1,468; 19; 10; 1 9. 3,899; 29; 11; 2 10. 4,987; 28; 10; 1

## Put in a Good Word for Me (page 150)

1. mayor; 2. sheriff; 3. sire;
4. earl; 5. cardinal; 6. captain;
7. pope; 8. lieutenant

## Add Another Word (page 151)

1. offside, office, offbeat, offend; 2. pardon, parrot, parking, parable; 3. subway, subdue, sublime, subside

## Crossword (pages 152–153)

## Clued In (page 154)

**Clues:** stand, ate, big, white, toast, art, row, well, mouth, rest
**Riddle box:** What ten-letter word starts with gas? Automobile.

## Hotel Pool Scene (page 155)

Our answers (other answers are possible)
1. These start with S: sandals, seagull, soda, sunglasses, sunscreen, surfboard, swimming, swimsuit
2. Things that are wrong: There's a tree in the pool; there's a fish in the pool; there are air bubbles coming from the boy on the diving board; the lifeguard is facing the wrong way; and there's a surfboarder in the pool.
3. S-P-L-A-S-H

## Trivia Quiz (page 156)

1. Scrabble
2. Indigo
3. 46 + 27
4. Asia
5. Soles of the feet
6. Winter Olympics

### Tarzanna's Treehouse (page 157)

### Confused Compounds (page 158)

1. ladybug; 2. upset;
3. shortcut; 4. weekend;
5. outfit; 6. underground;
7. handstand; 8. backfire;
9. nightgown; 10. flashlight;
11. tightrope; 12. blacktop;
13. slowpoke; 14. farewell;
15. faraway; 16. stoplight

### Music Makers (page 159)

### Famous Americans (page 160)

1. Elvis Presley; 2. Marilyn
Monroe; 3. Hank Aaron;
4. Toni Morrison; 5. George
Washington; 6. Eleanor
Roosevelt

### Categories (page 161)

Our answers (other answers
are possible): Fruits: banana;
cantaloupe, cherry; grape;
strawberry
Musical instruments:
accordion, alto saxophone,
autoharp; bagpipes, banjo,
bass drum, bass guitar,
bassoon, bugle; cello, cymbals,
clarinet; guitar, gong;
saxophone, snare drum,
sousaphone
Family relatives: aunt;
brother, brother-in-law;
cousin; granddaughter,
grandfather, grandmother,
grandnephew, grandniece,
grandson, great-aunt, great-
nephew, great-niece, great-
uncle; sister, sister-in-law, son,
stepdaughter, stepfather,
stepmother, stepson
4-letter words ending in Y:
achy, ahoy, airy, ally, army,
away; baby, body, bony, bray,
buoy, bury, busy; city, clay,
copy, cozy; gory, gray; slay,
stay, sway

### Clued In (page 162)

right, soft, sits, win, golf, test,
bat, nose, hands
Joke box: Who brings gifts to
the dentist? Santa Floss.

### Paint a Picture (page 163)

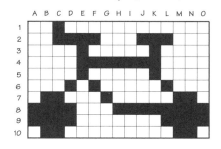

bicycle

### Three-Letter Challenge (page 164)

1. off, try, gas, ant, ice, web,
France; 2. fir, ore, eel, all, was,
end, add, Ireland; 3. pen, age,
dye, spy, ate, Egypt; 4. are,
cup, use, ask, pig, can, Russia;
5. sty, the, jar, rid, fly, mat,
one, add, Thailand

### Troubles at Home (page 165)

1. car; 2. chimney;
3. doorknob; 4. jump rope;
5. lawnmower's wheels;
6. missing "5"; 7. tree's leaves;
8. wagon's handles; 9. water
from hose; 10. weather vane
(to name a few)

### True/False (page 166)

1. true-L; 2. true-E; 3. true-M;
4. false-O; 5. true-N;
6. false-Y; 7. true-S; 8. false-
N; 9. false-I; 10. true-C;
11. true-K; 12. false-E;
13. true-T;
**Children's author:** Lemony
Snicket

## School Daze (page 167)

1. testing; 2. physical education; 3. show and tell; 4. study hall; 5. foreign language; 6. chalkboard; 7. report card; 8. elementary school; 9. kindergarten; 10. substitute teacher; 11. penmanship; 12. research paper

## Start/Finish Rhymes (page 168)

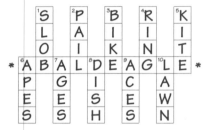

Riddle answer: A bald eagle

## Letters and Shapes (page 169)

1. grain, ring, ran, air
2. clear, real, lace, car

## A Word Train (page 170)

1. Africa; 2. cafe; 3. feet; 4. ethnic; 5. icicle; 6. letter; 7. error; 8. orange; 9. genuine; 10. nest; 11. staid; 12. idol; 13. olive; 14. veteran; 15. answer

## Take Note (page 171)

**Answer:** To pick up some rapping paper

## Moving Around (page 172)

1. ton; 2. ant; 3. ear or era; 4. tip; 5. felt; 6. leap or plea; 7. went; 8. door; 9. sneak; 10. cloud; 11. thorn; 12. shout; 13. board; 14. leash; 15. steam or mates or tames; 16. tears or rates

## Two Magic Squares (page 173)

| ¹C | ²H | ³I | ⁴P |
|---|---|---|---|
| ²H | E | R | O |
| ³I | R | O | N |
| ⁴P | O | N | Y |

| ¹S | ²T | ³A | ⁴R |
|---|---|---|---|
| ²T | O | G | A |
| ³A | G | E | S |
| ⁴R | A | S | H |

## Let's Get Together (page 174)

1. kitten; 2. carrot; 3. mango; 4. satin; 5. button; 6. anthem; 7. robin; 8. portable; 9. proverb; 10. hammock

## Beam In on Bs (page 175)

baby, backpack, bag, ballerina, balloon, banana, bandana, baseball, basket, bat, bear, beard, bell, belt, bench, beret, bicycle, bird, blanket, blimp, boat, bone, book, boomerang, boots, bottle, bowling ball, bow tie, box, boxer, brain, branch, bread, bricks, broom, brush, bucket, bug, buildings, bull, bus, bush, butterfly

## Forward and Backward (page 176)

1. dad; 2. pop; 3. bib; 4. eye; 5. did; 6. pup; 7. gag; 8. noon; 9. deed; 10. level; 11. kayak; 12. radar

## Loony Limericks (page 177)

1. The weatherman rarely was RIGHT, So he said on the newscast one NIGHT: "I predict we'll see SNOW, But I really don't KNOW If things will turn out all WHITE."
2. "Come look at this pony I FOUND!" Said a girl to a boy who just FROWNED. He said, "Tell me the TRUTH, Is that really so, RUTH, Or are you just horsing AROUND?"

### Mountains of Fun (page 178)

### Extreme Trivia Quiz (page 179)

1. Cleopatra; 2. jet plane;
3. China; 4. Saturn;
5. 1 laptop computer;
6. Tiger Woods

### The State of AEIOU (page 180)

1. Indiana; 2. Oregon;
3. Alabama; 4. Mississippi;
5. California; 6. Texas;
7. Tennessee; 8. Maine;
9. Vermont; 10. Virginia;
11. Oklahoma; 12. Arizona;
13. Florida; 14. Kentucky;
15. Georgia; 16. Connecticut;
17. Idaho; 18. Montana;
19. Nebraska; 20. Illinois

### Bible Villains (page 181)

### Plurals (page 182)

1. mice; 2. men; 3. geese;
4. feet; 5. sheep; 6. leaves;
7. knives; 8. wolves; 9. calves;
10. deer; 11. women;
12. elves; 13. scissors;
14. lives

### Mix and Match Once Again (page 183)

1. stagecoach,
2. extraordinary,
3. pleasure, 4. horseshoe,
5. coastline; 1. cheapskate,
2. creation or reaction,
3. regardless, 4. nightmare,
5. battlefield; 1. limestone,
2. mastermind, 3. spreadsheet,
4. superman, 5. friendship

### Here's the Scoop (page 184)

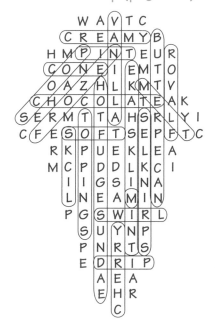

The uncircled letters spell out: "Watch me make my ice cream disappear!"

### Fivers (page 185)

Scary Halloween Costumes:
1. ghost; 2. alien; 3. witch;
4. devil; 5. mummy
Mammals: 1. tiger; 2. horse;
3. zebra; 4. camel; 5. skunk

### Fun with Opposites (page 186)

1. pouted; 2. frighten;
3. slower; 4. muffin;
5. bold; 6. Copenhagen;
7. pupil; 8. fender; 9. drawer;
10. gloves; 11. twine;
12. pullet; 13. breakfast;
14. Saturn; 15. Halloween

### Shake It Up (page 187)

### Trading Places (page 188)

1. bed, cot; 2. food, meat;
3. dog, pet; 4. book, read;
5. tree, bark; 6. fire, heat;
7. stars, shine; 8. buy, sell;
9. hat, head; 10. bread, loaf

### Age Puzzlers (page 189)

1. Kelcie–10
   Kelcie's mom–30
   Kelcie's grandmother–60

2. Jenny–25
   Jamie–21

3. Peggy–19
   Jimmy–11

4. Andy–16
   Mandy–8
   Randy–4

## Heartbreaker Challenge (page 190)

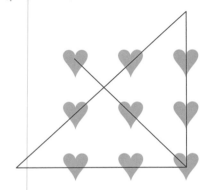

## Make-A-Word (page 191)

amputate, cabinet, cannonball, capital, catalog, doormat, heartache, informed, meadow, noontime, redhead, together

## Poetic License (page 192)

1. Why not?
2. See you soon
3. I hate you
4. Blue eyes
5. Peas and carrots
6. Be all that you can be
7. Wise guys
8. Making enemies
9. Are you up for it?
10. I'll be back

## A Lark in the Park (page 193)

1. left tree trunk; 2. woman's high heels; 3. baby carriage; 4. hand holding balloon; 5. statue with broom; 6. blimp; 7. earmuffs; 8. no kite tail; 9. jogger's shorts; 10. dog without spots; 11. cat with whiskers; 12. "NEWS"; 13. lamp post; 14. sitting boy with uncrossed legs; 15. jogger's ponytail

## Word Ladders (page 194)

1. GIVE
   HIVE
   HIKE
   BIKE
   BAKE
   TAKE
2. PASS
   PAWS
   PAWN
   PAIN
   PAIL
   FAIL
3. WORK
   CORK
   COOK
   COOP
   CLOP
   CLAP
   CLAY
   PLAY
4. HAND
   WAND
   WANT
   WART
   WARM
   FARM

FORM
FORT
FOOT

## Word Pyramids (page 195)

1.
```
        D
      E D
    D O E
  D O N E
D O Z E N
```

2.
```
        S
      I S
    S I T
  T I E S
E X I T S
```

3.
```
        A
      A M
    R A M
  A R M Y
M A Y O R
```

## Ships Ahoy! (page 196)

naval oranges

## Squished Countries (page 197)

1. Brazil/Poland
2. Greece/Lebanon
3. Australia/Cuba
4. Turkey/Vietnam
5. Venezuela/Switzerland
6. Singapore/Norway

7. Afghanistan/Bolivia
8. Belgium/Germany
9. Russia/Egypt
10. India/Honduras

## Selections (page 198)

1. control; 2. deleted;
3. employee; 4. informal;
5. intrudes; 6. ivory;
7. overture; 8. permanent;
9. quarreled; 10. scaffold;
11. thrive; 12. ventilate

## Hidden Meanings (page 199)

1. crossroads; 2. turn of the century; 3. growing pains;
4. long underwear;
5. smallpox; 6. scrambled eggs; 7. quit following me;
8. half an hour; 9. under the sea; 10. downtown;
11. leftover pizza;
12. checkup

## Unfinished Food (page 200)

1. grape; 2. prune; 3. cabbage;
4. Bermuda onion;
5. whipped cream;
6. nectarine; 7. spareribs;
8. steak; 9. lasagna; 10. tuna fish salad; 11. brownie;
12. clam chowder; 13. veal cutlet; 14. fried rice;
15. popcorn

## Yummy Partners (page 201)

1. cookies and milk; 2. apples and oranges; 3. crackers and cheese; 4. lemon and lime;
5. toast and jam; 6. soup and salad; 7. hamburger and fries;
8. spaghetti and meatballs;
9. bacon and eggs;
10. pancakes and syrup

## Wacky Wordies (page 202)

1. Little Red Riding Hood
2. Going on vacation
3. Order in the court
4. It's no big deal
5. I know a shortcut
6. Hole-in-one

## Word Magic (page 203)

1. book, boot, foot, fort, fork
2. page, cage, cane, cone, bone
3. well, wall, ball, bald, band

## Yes and No (page 204)

1. eyes; 2. shyest;
3. yesterday; 4. slyest;
5. eyesight; 6. dyes; 7. note;
8. north; 9. snow; 10. noise;
11. knock; 12. canoe;
13. cannon; 14. nonfiction

## Famous Men in the Bible (page 205)

1. Peter; 2. Solomon; 3. Adam;
4. Nicodemus; 5. Abraham;
6. Noah; 7. Judas; 8. Moses;
9. David; 10. Barnabas

## Crossword (pages 206–207)

## On Top of Spaghetti (page 208)

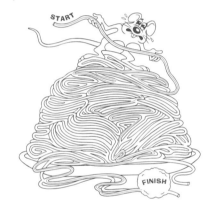

## Rhyme Time (page 209)

1. bright; 2. castle; 3. drool;
4. frown; 5. gravity;
6. handstand; 7. jockey;
8. knew; 9. laughter;
10. mixed; 11. prize; 12. ride;
13. smallest; 14. thirty;
15. Viking; 16. while

## Going for the Green (page 210)

## Letter Perfect (page 211)

1. athlete; 2. ballet;
3. booklet; 4. bracelet;
5. lettuce; 6. mistletoe;
7. omelet; 8. scarlet;
9. skeleton; 10. skillet;
11. triplets; 12. violet;
13. wallet

## You're Precious (page 212)

She was looking for a naval ring.

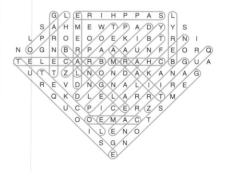

## Add Another Word (page 213)

1. baron, barbell, barking, barred; 2. Antarctic, anthem, antelope, antacid; 3. capsize, capable, caprice, capstone

## Start at the End (page 214)

1. rainbow/bowling
2. happen/pencil
3. spear/earring
4. orbit/bitten
5. whiffed/federal
6. pumpkin/kindly
7. sunset/settler
8. teacup/cupid
9. heart/article
10. bishop/hopeful
11. catalog/logical
12. caravan/vanish

## Amusement Park (page 215)

1. These don't belong: cow on Ferris wheel, lawn mower, chair, frying pan, telephone.
2. These start with R: radio, ruler, rabbit, ring, rake.
3. These are hidden: pencil, spoon, baseball bat.

## Scrambled Synonyms (page 216)

1. meadow & field; 2. guest & visitor; 3. trash & garbage; 4. cold & chilly; 5. rain & pour; 6. neat & tidy; 7. dirty & filthy; 8. shout & scream; 9. smart & clever; 10. pretty & cute; 11. lady & woman; 12. writer & author

## Measuring Up (page 217)

## Eye Rhymes (page 218)

1. war; 2. watch; 3. have; 4. wash; 5. worth; 6. golf; 7. plow; 8. weight; 9. horse; 10. tease; 11. done & gone; 12. lose & dose

## Find-a-President (page 219)

1. If I take the BUS, How long will it take to get to the White House? 2. I am awaRE A GANder followed a goose and ended up at the farm. 3. Should we do the WASHING TONight or tomorrow? 4. Pirates senT RUM ANd gold home to their families. 5. What makes JOHN SO Nervous? 6. I'm glAD AMSterdam's tulips are blooming early. 7. Take the CAR, TERry, and I'll meet you there. 8. In SoHO, OVER the lake flew the wild geese. 9. That kind of pool is sunKEN, NED. You can't put it above ground. 10. CLINT ONly eats the Idaho potatoes his father grows. 11. Times are HARD IN Ghost towns.

## Crossword (pages 220–221)

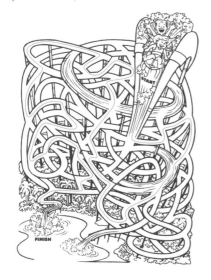

| | | | | | | | | | |
|---|---|---|---|---|---|---|---|---|---|
| A | T | M | | A | R | T | | C | U | P |

(crossword grid reading)

Row 1: A T M | A R T | C U P
Row 2: O W E | B A A | A S A
Row 3: L O T S O F M O N E Y
Row 4: E N T E R
Row 5: P L A T E | D E N T S
Row 6: J E T | B O O
Row 7: S T E P S | S O A P Y
Row 8: A L T A R
Row 9: M I L L I O N A I R E
Row 10: O N A | M A D | D A Y
Row 11: W A G | Y D S | O N E

## Wild Wally's Waterpark (page 222)

## Going Ape (page 223)

1. Chapel; 2. Drapes;
3. Shapes; 4. Landscape;
5. Grapes; 6. Lapel;
7. Scrape; 8. Heaped;
9. Reaped; 10. Taped;
11. Escape; 12. Paper

## Fivers (page 224)

Drinks: 1. water; 2. punch;
3. cider; 4. juice; 5. cocoa.
Fruits: 1. apple; 2. grape;
3. lemon; 4. melon; 5. berry.

## Partials (page 225)

1. judo/dough
2. arrive/venom
3. smash/shelf
4. ordeal/alike
5. drizzle/leopard
6. sketch/choose
7. debate/terrify
8. pretty/typhoon
9. manage/general
10. horrid/ideal
11. hyena/natural
12. knife/feeble

## Crisscross Connection (page 226)

### Languages

```
CHINESE        J
Z              A
ENGLISH        P
C    A         A
H    ITALIAN   N
     I         E
SPANISH        S
               E
```

### Fabrics

```
BROCADE
U
R     D
LINEN      S
A  N   V   A
P  I   E   T
   MUSLIN  I
       L   N
       V
       E
POLYESTER
```

## Tools

```
SAW
T     W
A     R        L
PLIERSANDER    E
L     N        V
E     C   DRILL E
R     H   E    L
HAMMER
```

## Fun with Idioms (page 227)

1. apple; 2. hat; 3. black
sheep; 4. world; 5. butterflies;
6. bucket; 7. cake; 8. roof;
9. kite; 10. books; 11. fish;
12. moon

## Number Squares (page 228)

1.

| 9 | 4 | 2 |
|---|---|---|
| 5 | 3 | 7 |
| 1 | 8 | 6 |

2.

| 8 | 1 | 3 |
|---|---|---|
| 0 | 5 | 7 |
| 4 | 6 | 2 |

## Number Challenge (page 229)

| | | | | |
|---|---|---|---|---|
| 2 5 | | | 1 2 5 | |
| 2 1 | | 2 6 2 5 | | |
| 2 0 2 5 | | | 4 2 | |
| | 3 2 4 | | | |
| 4 4 | | 1 9 3 6 | | |
| 2 0 2 2 | | | 6 3 | |
| 2 4 9 | | 6 7 | | |

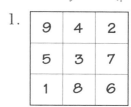

## Body Language (page 230)

1. handbag; 2. football; 3. fingerprint; 4. wristwatch; 5. earphone; 6. eyeglasses; 7. lipstick; 8. necktie; 9. headlight; 10. mouthpiece; 11. armchair; 12. backpack

## Whose Flag Is That? (page 231)

1. Canada; 2. Mexico; 3. China; 4. Turkey; 5. Brazil; 6. Australia; 7. Japan; 8. Liberia

## Relations (pages 232–233)

1. milk, coffee, tea; beverages; 2. story, book, poem; things you read; 3. car, bus, van; vehicles; 4. corn, bean, carrot; vegetables; 5. Bart, Lisa, Homer; Simpson family members; 6. March, June, July; months; 7. chair, bench, sofa; things you sit on; 8. spade, heart, club; card suits; 9. mouse, modem, printer; things connected to a computer; 10. Paris, Rome, Berlin; European cities

## Crossword (pages 234–235)

## Search for Ss (page 236)

sailboat, sand, sandals, sandcastle, scarf, sea, seagull, seal, seashell, seven, shark, ship, shirt, shorts, shovel, six, skeleton, skunk, smiley face, snail, snake, snowperson, sock, sombrero, spider, spoon, square, squirrel, stamp, starfish, stars, stegosaurus, stereo, storm, strawberry, stripes, sunflower, sunset, swan, swimmer

## Word Pyramids (page 237)

1. t, at, ate, seat, takes, skater, darkest

2. o, on, not, note, stone, honest, thrones, southern

## Frame-Up (page 238)

## You've Got Mail! (page 239)

1. W/OR/MS
2. MA/ID
3. I/NH/AL/E
4. CA/TN/IP
5. C/AR RI/DE
6. C/HI/MN/EY
7. CO/OK/BO/OK
8. D/IA/MO/ND
9. CO/M/PA/NY
10. NE/CT/AR/IN/E

## Crossword (pages 240–241)

## Scrambled States (page 242)

1. Massachusetts; 2. Pennsylvania; 3. Virginia; 4. Connecticut; 5. Georgia; 6. Maryland; 7. Rhode Island; 8. North Carolina; 9. New Hampshire; 10. Vermont; 11. New York; 12. New Jersey They were 12 of the 13 first states to form the United States.

## Presidential Nicknames (page 243)

1. Zachary Taylor
2. Thomas Jefferson
3. Grover Cleveland
4. Jimmy Carter
5. Theodore Roosevelt
6. Benjamin Harrison
7. Calvin Coolidge
8. Ronald Reagan
9. Andrew Jackson
10. John Quincy Adams

## Guess the Theme (pages 244–245)

ache, bare, board, breaker, diamond, feed, field, flash, ground, hand, horse, hunch, laid, pack, paper, piggy, quarter, stroke, talk, yard. Theme: Add "back" to the front or back of each word for a new word.

## Some Dom Questions (page 246)

1. freedom; 2. wisdom;
3. boredom; 4. kingdom;
5. seldom; 6. random;
7. stardom

## Once Around the Block (page 247)

## Blended Words (page 248)

1. flare; 2. squiggle;
3. pang; 4. motel;
5. swipe; 6. blurt;
7. brunch; 8. flop;
9. waddle; 10. splurge;
11. camcorder

## Eagle Eyes (page 249)

A farmer

## Double Wacky Wordies (page 250)

1. Going around in circles
2. Side by side
3. Jumping up and down
4. Double play
5. *Hollywood Squares*
6. Over and over again

## Amazing Number Pyramid (page 251)

1
11
111
1,111
11,111
111,111
1,111,111
11,111,111
111,111,111

The number of digits increases by one each time, and the only digit in each answer is 1.

## Crossword (pages 252–253)

## Something's Missing (page 254)

**Message:** Absence makes the heart grow fonder.

## What's Wrong in Time? (page 255)

basketball court, car, flying disc, inline skates, laptop computer, mountain bike, pay phone, stop sign, streetlight, televisions

## Computer Know-How (page 256)

1. boot; 2. crash; 3. launch;
4. menu; 5. mouse; 6. printer;
7. paste; 8. virus; 9. ram;
10. scanner
**Answer to riddle:** microchips

## Sixes and Sevens (page 257)

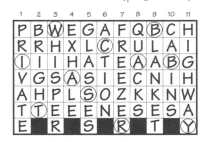

**Answer to riddle:** It was crabby.

## Once Around the Big Block (page 258)

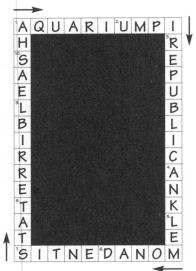

## Palindrome Search (page 259)

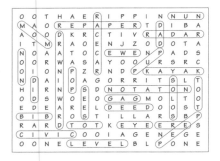

## Three in a Row (page 260)

1. first; 2. laughing; 3. defeat;
4. study; 5. hijack;
6. unopened; 7. afghan;
8. worst; 9. pony; 10. golfed;
11. peanuts; 12. respond

## Mixed Messages (page 261)

1. a rainbow; 2. a tot rod;
3. gloves

## Crossword (pages 262–263)

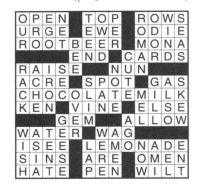

## You've Got Mail! (page 264)

1. B/AL/L GA/ME
2. M/IL/KS
3. R/AZ/OR
4. FL/AK/E
5. HI/DE/O/UT
6. DE/SC/RI/BE
7. CO/CA-CO/LA
8. MI/SD/E/AL
9. NO VA/CA/NC/Y
10. WI/ND/OW/PA/NE

## Number Patterns (page 265)

1. 56, 67, 78 (Both digits increase by 1 each time.)
2. 21, 28, 36 (Add 1, add 2, add 3, add 4, and so on.)
3. 64, 73, 82 (The tens increase by 1 each time, and the ones decrease by 1.)
4. 17, 16, 21 (Add 5 to the first number, and subtract 1 from the next number.)
5. 5, 25, 6 (A number is followed by its square.)
6. 21, 34, 55 (Each number is added to the one before it.)
7. One digit is twice the other digit; the numbers are divisible by 3.
8. The two outer digits add up to the middle digit.
9. The middle digit is half the sum of the outer digits.

## Finish Lines (page 266)

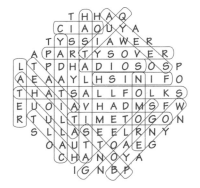

The leftover letters spell: "That's a wrap. Hope you had fun. See you again."